BEYOND
GOODBYE

HEALING, HONORING,
AND RECONNECTING AFTER PET LOSS

A Comprehensive Guide to Grieving, Remembering,
and Finding Peace After the Death of a Beloved Pet

BEN WHITLOW

Please join our mailing list to learn
about new and upcoming books by Ben Whitlow.

BEN WHITLOW

CONTENTS

PART V:
GUIDED REFLECTIONS
AND HEALING ACTIVITIES

INTRODUCTION
WHY PET GRIEF MATTERS

Although the house was quiet, it did not have a sense of tranquility. It is the kind of silence that grows stronger after a loss. A silence formerly filled by gentle paws moving over the floor, the rhythmic jingle of a collar, and the sighs of a buddy sleeping next to you. In the kitchen, Maya was standing there making a second cup of coffee that she would never be able to finish. The passing of her golden retriever, Cooper, who was twelve years old, had occurred just three days prior, and her world had been turned upside down. It was not simply the daily routines but the emotional anchor she had constructed her life around without realizing it. There had been communications from friends. Some people are friendly, while others are awkward. The message read, "You'll get another one." She pondered the message for a long time—not because it helped, but because it hurt. It dismissed her sorrow as fleeting as if it held little weight. But no one could substitute for Cooper.

This space is familiar to you if you have ever loved an animal, and I mean that in a genuine sense. Emptiness, pain, and a desire for one more nose, nuzzle, or tail wag are all experienced feelings. You know their absence creates a void in your day and your heart. You search for them in the nooks and crannies of your house, in the routines you regularly engage in, and in the manner that sunlight still reaches where they used to sleep. When people say things like, "It's just a pet," it doesn't simply hurt; it hurts deeply. It gives you the impression that you are not visible.

When a dear animal companion passes away, the loss that follows is sometimes a quiet type of grief. Even though society reserves intense grieving for human relationships, people rarely discuss it because cultural conventions have overshadowed it. Nevertheless, love follows no set hierarchy, as everyone who has ever shared life with a pet knows all too well. All love is love. Defeat is a loss. And the pain that comes after the breakup of that link is just as genuine, unfiltered, and deserving of compassion as the grief that comes before it.

It is not yet the case that society has entirely accepted that reality. Recognizing animals that provide emotional support, celebrating birthdays for pets, and even creating social media profiles in their names are all examples of how far we have come. However, when that pet passes away, there is still a widespread unease with the concept of grieving them as completely as possible. There is a message that might be subtle, or sometimes it can be obvious, and it says, "Move on. You are making an excessive amount of this." It is a grieving that is not recognized by the public or supported by society, and it is a form of disenfranchised grief. People may experience feelings of isolation at precisely the moment when they require the support of a group the most.

We can attribute much of the intensity of this grieving to the profound significance our pets hold in our lives. They are not just animals. They walk beside us as companions, witness our everyday moments, and quietly support us through our best and most challenging times. They don't judge us. They don't hold grudges. They continue to show up with love, loyalty, and presence that is consistent with their presence. They shape our identities in some way. To some people, they are the only source of love that is not conditional, as they have never experienced it. Some people find solace in them after experiencing a traumatic event, stability amid mental health issues, or the beating heart of their household. It is not simply a pet absent when that presence is suddenly gone; it is something else entirely. Yes, it is safe. This is a routine. The self is a component of it.

When someone loses a pet, they frequently experience guilt—remorse for choices taken, ignoring warning signs, and wasting time. The emotional burden may be intolerable, particularly in situations involving euthanasia. You might wonder, "Did I make the right decision?" The question, "What if I had waited one more day?" When love is profound, responsibility also becomes profound. However, the absence of suffering is not a criterion for determining love. We measure love by presence—by showing up daily to care, soothe, and connect with others.

For those individuals who are still showing up, this book is for you. This is for anyone walking the delicate path between memory and healing. It's for those who have heard that their grief doesn't matter—or have come to believe they should already be "over it."

Everyone who has ever grieved into a pet's hair laughed at their peculiarities, or whispered secrets into ears that never judged them is the recipient of this collection. This book is for you if you have ever uttered something like "They were more than just a pet."

Take, for example, the story of Reuben, a widower who is 67 years old and lives in a peaceful agricultural community. It was his cat, Junebug, who provided him with a reason to get out of bed every morning after the death of his wife. While he was reading, she would curl up next to him and sit on his chest. When he watched television, she would sit on his chest and meow until he fed her at 7:15 in the morning. In the aftermath of her passing due to kidney failure, Reuben was utterly heartbroken, but he was reluctant to express to anyone how profoundly it affected him. His children expressed their regrets, but his neighbor, who shrugged and muttered, "You'll get used to it," did not give any words of support. One of Reuben's goals was to avoid "getting used to it." He wanted the freedom to grieve. Eventually, he found a small online support group for pet loss. In that space, he shared his pain with strangers and, in return, received validation. People acknowledged his love and honored his sorrow. Through small rituals, weekly letters, and photo tributes, he slowly began to make sense of the feelings he had been keeping inside. These practices didn't erase his loss, but they helped him carry it in a safe, meaningful way.

When a pet dies, society often fails to offer the usual rituals we use to honor other kinds of loss. Funerals rarely happen. Workplaces don't offer bereavement leave. No one publishes obituaries for pets. Yet the pain can cut just as deeply—sometimes even more—because it lacks validation. We see their favorite treat in the store and feel a wave of sadness we must shoulder in silence, unsure if it's okay to grieve in the grocery aisle. We question whether keeping their toys or framing their picture makes us seem "ridiculous."

But you're not ridiculous. You're grieving. And that grief is sacred.

I wrote this book specifically for that moment—for you. It offers more than sympathy; it provides proper support. It doesn't claim one universal method because grief doesn't follow a straight path. It's not tidy. It's messy, unpredictable, and deeply personal.

In the chapters ahead, you'll explore the powerful bond between humans and pets and why their absence leaves such a profound emptiness. You'll gain insight into the emotional, psychological, and even physical impact of losing a beloved animal, along with the myths that often surround this kind of grief. We'll navigate the full spectrum of emotion—from guilt and anger to unexpected joy and quiet shame. Along the way, you'll hear authentic voices from others who have walked this road and found meaning again.

You'll also receive tools—not fixed instructions, but gentle prompts, practices, and rituals you can tailor to your journey. You might write a letter, create art, light a candle each night, make a photo book, plant a tree, or speak softly to your beloved pet when no one else is listening. Every one of these acts is valid. There's no wrong way to honor the soul who brightened your life.

The book also explores what comes next—not in the sense of "moving on," but instead "moving forward with" your loss. You might wonder if—or when—you'll feel ready to open your heart to another animal. Or you might want to learn how to keep a spiritual or emotional connection with the one you lost. Grief doesn't disappear; it transforms. It softens. It weaves itself into the fabric of your life, becoming a quiet part of your growth.

For families with multiple pets, you'll find guidance on how to help partners, children, and surviving pets process the loss together. If grief has isolated you—if your pet was your only thread of connection—this book offers gentle ways back into the community, even if just one kind voice at a time.

Nothing in these pages can replace the one you lost. That's not the goal. The goal is to affirm that your sorrow is genuine, your love is deep, and your healing matters.

You might feel like you're simply having a conversation as you read. That's intentional. You don't need clinical definitions or distant theories. You need understanding. You need someone to sit beside you in the pain and say, "I get it. I've been there. You're not alone."

Grief will surprise you along the way. One day, you may smile gently when you find your pet's hair still clinging to your favorite sweater. You may laugh at a memory of your cat's strange quirks. These aren't setbacks—they're signs that love lives on.

In time, the pain that feels unbearable today may turn into something you can hold—not as a weight, but as a tribute. And when that shift happens, you'll see that your love didn't die with your loss. It became even more visible.

So, take your time with this. Read at your own pace. Skip around. Revisit chapters. Scribble notes in the margins. Let these pages be your companion, comfort, and guide when everything else feels too heavy. When you grieve a pet, you don't break—you show your humanity. You begin to heal. And even though you can't see the one you lost, your bond with them remains unshakably real.

REFLECTIONS & NEXT STEPS

- What part of your grief feels the hardest to name right now?
- Is there someone in your life who has dismissed your grief? How did that make you feel?
- Can you think of a moment—big or small—that shows how much your pet meant to you?
- Find a quiet place today. Say their name out loud. Let yourself feel whatever comes.

In the chapters, we'll explore that bond, look grief in the eye, and begin the slow, gentle journey toward remembering without pain. You're not alone—and you don't have to rush. Let's start together.

PART I
UNDERSTANDING
THE BOND AND THE LOSS

CHAPTER 1
WHY OUR PETS MEAN SO MUCH

The revelation that the leash had been left unattended by the door for the first time was shocking. In the past, that simple item had played a role in a cherished daily rhythm—the jingling sounds that sparked anticipation, the joyful tapping of paws, the creak of the door swinging open, and the shared steps that followed into the fresh air. But now, the leash hung silently, untouched. In that stillness, reality began to settle in. Something wasn't just missing. Someone was.

The loss of a pet devastates many more deeply than they ever expected. It's not just the death of an animal—it's the end of a relationship built on unconditional love. This bond forms through time, touch, presence, sound, and trust. For many, the emotional connection with a pet feels more secure than any human relationship. That doesn't mean people don't love each other deeply—but the love we receive from pets comes with a steady, wordless reassurance. It's always there. That unwavering loyalty weaves pets into the fabric of our lives, anchoring our days with their presence and making them essential to our routines.

More Than a Pet: They Are Family

When people refer to their pets as "my dog," "my cat," or "my bird," they rarely mean to refer to their possessions. The companions in question are not only accessories; instead, they are members of the family. They accompany us through the peaceful in-betweens of life, console us when we are experiencing pain, and join us in celebrating our victories. We see this reflected in the way people speak to their pets—through nicknames, daily routines, bedtime rituals, and even including them in family photos. Many pets hold the same emotional presence and weight as a sibling or child might for someone else.

Their existence eventually gets ingrained in the routine. When I woke up, I found furry paws on the bed—preparing the food while simultaneously sensing eyes that wanted a bite in silence. When someone is at the door, you hear a bark that is recognizable to you. Having a warm body cuddled up at your feet while watching television. We may not see these as exceptional moments, but we fill them with deep significance. Pets enhance the structure. Even the things they require, such as feeding times, walks, and grooming, contribute to the day's peaceful rhythm. Moreover, when that rhythm stops, you feel like life has taken something vital from you.

Beyond the mundane, pets become integral to an individual's identity. Specific individuals are well-known in their communities because of their dogs. Several people like to embellish their houses with artwork depicting their parrots, while others designate a particular position on the couch for their rabbits. A pet is more than just an addition to your life—those who shape it. They partly shape the way we live and who we are.

THE BIOLOGY OF BONDING: WHY THE CONNECTION FEELS SO DEEP

The fact that these connections seem so powerful is due to a very real and literal physical reason. Oxytocin, sometimes known as the "love hormone," is released into our brains whenever we engage with pets, particularly when we touch them or make eye contact with other people. The hormone that is responsible for the bonding that occurs between mothers and their infants, between loving partners, and between close friends is the same molecule. It instills trust, warmth, and safety in the individual. This spike of oxytocin has the potential to lower blood pressure, slow the heart rate, and contribute to the development of emotional cohesion.

There is not a single side to this biological response. Several studies have demonstrated that dogs, for instance, experience a similar release of oxytocin whenever they view or engage with their preferred human. A mutually reinforcing structure exists. Every moment we spend together, every stare we exchange, and every petting session helps to develop the emotional circuitry that binds us together.

However, the bonding is not limited to biological terms. Their experiences mold people's emotional bonding with their dogs in life. Many people reconnect with their dogs during life's turning points—after a loss, while healing, or in times of change. Pets step in as steady companions and anchors within the family. And as time passes, that emotional bond deepens into something unshakable.

When individuals talk about their pets being their soulmates, they are not exaggerating the situation. With this title, the unspoken understanding, the effortless camaraderie, and the feeling that this being knows you not through words but through presence are all captured. Your energy, your voice, and your perfume are all very familiar to them. They learn your routines and the moods you are in. As a response, they either respond with a sense of intuitive comfort or excitement. A representation of your emotional life that is free of judgment, they become a mirror for your emotional life.

MENTAL HEALTH AND THE SILENT SUPPORT SYSTEM

The quiet therapists that pets are for many people. They provide a buffer against the harsh edges of life simply under their presence. Most of the time, animals can provide a grounding influence during times of worry, depression, or stress. They break the unproductive cycle of negative thought. Simplistic requirements, such as a stroll, a meal, or a light shove, are what they use to pull people out of downward spirals. The emotional space provided by their nonverbal support is conducive to healing.

Clinical investigations have shown that having a pet companion can lower cortisol levels—the hormone the body releases in response to stress. Experimenting with animals regularly can alleviate the symptoms of anxiety and potentially lessen the frequency of panic attacks. When people spend time with their pets, they report feeling more emotionally controlled, less lonely, and calmer than when they were elsewhere. A source of stability that does not rely on words or explanation, pets can become an integral part of a survival strategy for those who have post-traumatic stress disorder (PTSD), panic disorders, or chronic illnesses.

In addition, pets encourage the expression of emotions. People frequently confide in their pets when they have difficulty opening up to others, providing them with information regarding the day, weeping in their furry arms, and having a good time in their antics. These seemingly insignificant encounters add to something far more significant: establishing a secure environment where one can totally and unapologetically be themselves.

Children, especially, can gain from these kinds of relationships. Having a pet as a child teaches a person empathy, responsibility, and how to communicate effectively. Children growing up in unstable or challenging environments often find their first steady source of affection in a pet. Pets also provide older persons with a sense of purpose and company, which can be helpful in the face of feelings of isolation or cognitive impairment. Throughout a person's life, animals serve as more than just companions; they become lifelines.

THE UNMATCHED GIFT OF UNCONDITIONAL LOVE

Love that is not conditional is uncommon. The situation is frequently difficult by ego, miscommunication, or expectations. Pets, on the other hand, provide a unique quality. The love that they share does not require perfection. It is not necessary to give explanations. This is the case.

They are unconcerned about their status, appearance, or level of accomplishment. They don't hold onto resentment. They are quick to forgive, fast to welcome, and ready to return affection repeatedly. They rejoice at your return to your home as if you have triumphed over vast mountains. They are tolerant of your whims, your shortcomings, and your inconsistencies. The love of that kind transforms people. It smooths them out. It imparts knowledge to them.

The imprint of such love is left on a person when they experience it regularly, daily, over some years. There is more to the quiet than a lack of sound when that love is suddenly no longer present. Specifically, we long for the kind of acceptance that only a pet can offer.

Because of this, the grief that follows the death of a pet can feel so unsettling. It's not only about missing a friend or coworker. We mourn the loss of a sense of security and affection—a version of life made better by that loved one's presence. It is the end of the joy and emotional simplicity we experience daily. And for many, it is the loss of the only being who never judged them and saw them in their proper form.

Even in silence, our relationships with pets lose none of their depth. In many ways, they grow even more profound. These bonds don't rely on words—they grow from shared experiences. They form through time together, closeness, affection, and a mutual devotion that needs no translation.

Biology lays the groundwork for these relationships. Daily routines nurture them. Psychological connections keep them strong. Over time, they become essential threads in the fabric of daily life. So, when those threads unravel, it makes perfect sense that grief would follow—and that grief runs deep. There is no easy fix for that kind of loss.

We must first understand why our pets mean so much to us to begin the healing process. When we acknowledge how they've shaped our identity and supported our mental health, we validate the sorrow we feel when they're gone. In doing so, we also shine a light on the beauty of their presence.

As we move into the chapters, we'll explore how to navigate the tangled emotions of losing a beloved pet. We'll examine guilt and shame, the pain of sudden loss, and the long road to healing. Yet through it all, we'll return to one simple truth: they mattered. Their love was real. And your grief doesn't just make sense—it reflects the depth of the bond you shared.

Reflections & Next Steps

- What did your pet bring to your daily routine that you miss most?
- Can you describe a moment when their presence brought you unexpected comfort?
- How would you describe the kind of love you shared—if it could speak, what would it say?
- Write down three things your pet taught you. These lessons live on.

CHAPTER 2
WHAT MAKES PET GRIEF UNIQUE

After a certain point, the globe continues to turn, but you do not. In the middle of traffic, the car behind you honks. The delivery person displays a courteous grin. You are on the phone with someone telling you about their weekend. In the meantime, your entire world has come to a halt. You no longer have your pet, and for some reason, everything seems unexplainable. As you draw closer to your house, you can still hear their footsteps, feel their shape snuggled up next to you, and anticipate seeing them at the door. Nevertheless, they are not present. No one else seemed to be paying attention to this.

In this way, pet loss reveals a painful paradox. It feels intensely real and quietly devastating, yet the world often fails to see it. No one holds a formal ritual. Coworkers don't send sympathy cards. Employers don't offer a week off. Society usually overlooks this kind of mourning, leaving many grieving pet owners to suffer in silence.

GRIEVING IN THE SHADOWS: DISENFRANCHISED GRIEF

The loss of a pet is one of the most challenging sorts of loss to experience since it is not always accorded the same level of emotional license as other types of bereavement. "Disenfranchised grief" is a term used by psychologists to describe grief that is not openly acknowledged, socially supported, or publicly mourned. This type of sadness falls under this category. People are frequently taught, without their knowledge, that the amount of suffering they are experiencing is "too much" or "out of proportion."

People often deliver the message indirectly: *"It was just a dog." "You can always get another one." "At least it wasn't a person."* Though many intend these words to comfort, they often dismiss the depth of the loss, and the strength of the bond shared.

Because of this, many people learn to hide their pain. They cry in secret. They pretend they're okay. They carry something heavy with them and have no safe place to set it down.

Grief grows heavier when no one acknowledges it. Without validation, people begin to question themselves. *"Why can't I just move on?" "What's wrong with me?"* But the truth is—nothing is wrong with you. The sorrow isn't the problem. The silence surrounding it is.

WHAT PEOPLE DON'T SEE

There is more to pets than their outward appearance. Identities, rhythms, and memories are all intertwined with them. It is not just death that is the cause of their loss; rather, it is upheaval. No one greets you at the door anymore. No loyal steps follow you from room to room. You can no longer find comfort in a warm nuzzle or a familiar, understanding glance during challenging moments.

A common thing that people overlook is the constant presence of pets. They do not see the calm camaraderie, the gentle rituals, or the jokes that are only known to a select few. Without words, they cannot comprehend the extent of the emotional labor that pets consume. When you are in a state of brokenness, the way they sit next to you. The method in which they rejoice at your homecoming each time. The absence of that emotional presence gives the impression that it is so significant.

STORIES THAT REFLECT THE HIDDEN DEPTHS

One person kept a collar tucked inside their pillowcase for months. Another continued filling the food bowl each morning, unable to stop the habit. Someone else refused to vacuum the spot on the couch where fur still clung. These aren't symptoms of dysfunction. They're acts of love during loss. These behaviors reveal how grief shows up in quiet ways.

Many grieving pet parents speak of a moment when they accidentally called out their pet's name, expecting it to appear. The silence that followed was more painful than they could describe. That space—that is where the grief lives.

SUDDEN LOSS VS. ANTICIPATED LOSS

How a pet passes away can have an unanticipated impact on the grieving process. Accidents, unforeseen illnesses, and traumatic experiences are all examples of sudden losses that can cause shock. No one prepared for this. There's no farewell. Your mind struggles to grasp reality. You replay the last moment, again and again, trying to make sense of it. A wave of shock washes over you, leaving you stunned and hollow.

After an unexpected loss, your mind often floods with "what-ifs." *What if I had taken the day off and stayed home? What if I had noticed the signs sooner?* Searching for a different ending, your brain loops through every detail, desperately trying to rewrite the outcome. While this is a natural form of psychological self-protection, it often intensifies guilt and feelings of inadequacy.

Unexpected loss carries a different kind of sorrow than a loss you anticipate. When a pet faces a chronic illness or reaches old age, you have time to prepare. But that preparation comes with its price. Every new symptom, every change in medication, every trip to the vet starts a quiet countdown. You begin to grieve before the goodbye even arrives. That's anticipatory grief—the pain of loss before the loss.

Many people feel a complicated sense of relief when a prolonged illness ends. They feel relieved that their beloved companion no longer suffers. They feel relieved that the constant vigilance, the sleepless nights, and the emotional weight of care have ended. And then guilt creeps in. *Why do I feel better? Does this mean I didn't love them enough?*

But relief doesn't cancel love. It simply reflects the exhaustion from holding someone else's pain alongside your own. It's the body's quiet sigh after standing guard for so long. And that, too, is a form of love that asks nothing in return.

THE COMPLEXITY OF EUTHANASIA

The pain that a person experiences can take on a new dimension for individuals who have decided to put their pet to sleep. When it comes to suffering, compassion, and complexity, this is one of the most challenging decisions a pet parent can make. The decision to end suffering is frequently the most significant act of love; nonetheless, it can feel like a betrayal.

There is a lot of struggle with the time. Was it too soon to do so? "Did I wait for long enough?" They play back the last sight, the last touch, and the last breath taken. At that moment, people wondered if their pets knew how deeply they were loved. They doubt whether or not they made the correct decision even though all indications point in the right direction.

The loss of a pet carries with it a particular emotional burden. Hospice care for humans typically involves the patient or the medical team making decisions about the patient's care. Regarding pets, however, the obligation is entirely on the shoulders of the individual who loves them the most. People can be haunted by that obligation long after the moment has passed.

On the other hand, euthanasia is frequently a compassionate gesture. Love is what decides to choose peace over suffering. When confronted with an intolerable decision, it requires bravery. And it is the kind of thing that should be acknowledged, not only as a loss but also as an act of love.

DIFFERENT PEOPLE, DIFFERENT GRIEF

Every person uniquely experiences grief. In addition, this is especially true regarding the loss of a pet. For instance, the death of a pet is frequently the first time that children genuinely come into contact with the concept of death. They may lack the vocabulary to express their melancholy adequately, but they strongly feel it. They may persist in asking questions, act out, or become abnormally silent. Some people may be concerned that they have done something wrong. Those exposed to various types of separation could acquire a phobia of them.

Adults of a more advanced age face a distinct issue. Some people consider their pet to be their primary companion. The person who eats meals spends days and sleeps together. Whoever is responsible for providing time with order and significance. When a pet dies, the resulting sense of isolation can be severe. Older individuals may suffer in silence if they do not have a social network that is familiar with the experience of losing a pet.

Individuals living with disabilities or chronic illnesses often feel a profound sense of loss when they lose a pet. Not only do their dogs act as companions, but they also frequently function as forms of emotional and even physical support for them. When that support disappears, it can trigger a domino effect that impacts a person's health, safety, and overall well-being.

Those who work in veterinary medicine, animal shelters, or rescue organizations often experience what's known as "accumulative grief." Over time, they form bonds with many animals—and lose many. This ongoing cycle of love and loss can take a heavy emotional toll. Paired with the constant caregiving responsibility, it can lead to compassion fatigue and burnout.

Grieving Without a Roadmap

Because society rarely acknowledges pet loss, many people don't know what to expect. Some wonder if they're being "too emotional" or worry that their sadness isn't "normal." But grief doesn't follow a fixed pattern. Give me one moment, and you might feel perfectly fine. The next, a single memory might cause everything to fall apart. And that's not a sign that something is wrong—it's part of grieving. You're not just mourning; you're learning to carry the pieces of something that once felt whole.

No one follows a set timeline. No "right way" exists. No manual tells you how long it should take to heal. Some people welcome a new pet soon after their loss. Others wait months or even years. Some hold onto every collar, toy, and photograph. Others choose to give everything away. Every choice holds value—when you make it with intention and care.

Why This Grief Deserves a Name

It may not appear to be the same as other types of loss, but the grief that comes with losing a pet is just as real. It originates in profound emotional attachment, is molded by love, and is made more convoluted by society's silence. Because of this, it is deserving of recognition. As a result, it requires some room.

No, naming this sadness does not make it more intense; instead, it seems less isolated. It prompts compassion.

In doing so, it paves the way for healing. Because of this, it is OK for other people to say, "Yes, I felt that too."

The cost of love is the gift of grief. In addition, when our love for our animal companions is as profound as it is with ourselves, our sorrow will be equally profound. That is not a lack of strength. This is the truth.

REFLECTIONS & NEXT STEPS

- Have you ever felt dismissed or misunderstood while grieving a pet? What did you wish people had said instead?
- What type of loss did you experience—sudden, anticipated, or through euthanasia? What was the most challenging part?
- If you've been holding onto guilt, name it. Then, ask: "Would my pet want me to carry this pain?"
- Write down three ways your grief has surprised you—emotionally, physically, or mentally.

CHAPTER 3
TYPES OF LOSS
& WHO THIS BOOK HELPS

The house seemed oddly silent in its surroundings. It wasn't the kind of silence you discover when you're at rest; instead, it was a stillness that put pressure on the chest. The toys still sat in the corner of the room. The food dish stayed empty. No one called to be let back in, and no vet bills showed up in the mail. All that remained was a heavy, aching sense that something fundamental was missing—while the world moved on, unchanged as if nothing had happened.

No one experiences pet loss in the same way. Sometimes, it strikes suddenly. Other times, it unfolds slowly or becomes complicated by outside circumstances. For some, grief stems not from death itself but from a separation forced by life events beyond their control. Just as every life is unique, so is every goodbye. The way each person loses their animal companion reflects the distinct journey they've shared.

When it comes to grieving, there is no one "right" method to do it, and no one's experience of loss is more or less valid than another. It is essential to recognize that each of these types of loss can cause a great deal of pain and that each of them is deserving of medical attention, emotional support, and compassion.

SUDDEN LOSS: WHEN GOODBYE COMES WITHOUT WARNING

The unexpected passing of a pet is one of the most upsetting sorts of loss. Incidents such as an accident, an illness that was not anticipated, or a medical emergency that escalated too rapidly are situations that occur without prior planning and leave behind a state of emotional shock.

A sense of disbelief frequently characterizes the subsequent days. The brain has a hard time agreeing with what has taken place. In one instant, your pet was in good health, present, and happy; in the next, they were no longer there. You might have the impression that you were unable to say goodbye. Recalling events to locate when something may have been altered is possible.

Many individuals who are grieving the loss of a loved one can have intrusive thoughts or feelings of guilt. Why was it that I failed to notice the signs? "What would have happened if I had taken them in earlier?" Painful as they may be these ideas are very normal. It is love, not failure, that they represent.

Shock can make everything appear unreal. The grief may take a little longer to become apparent because the mind has not yet completely absorbed the fact. Be patient with yourself if this is something that you have experienced. The world is changing at an unsustainable rate, and your heart is attempting to keep up with it.

EUTHANASIA AND CHRONIC ILLNESS: THE LONG GOODBYE

The process of loss is gradual for some people. A pet will eventually become older, slow down, and exhibit indications of decline. The onset of chronic sickness occurs. Changes in diet, trips to the veterinarian, and medication are all things that become a regular part of life. The next step is the most challenging decision: determining when to let go.

Although euthanasia is an act of love, it does not feel like it at the time it is being performed. This choice was made out of a place of mercy, but it also comes with unbelievable grief. There are a lot of people who struggle with this obligation because they are afraid that they are playing God or that they have let down their pet.

Grief in these kinds of circumstances frequently starts before the parting of ways. A term for this phenomenon is anticipatory grief. When your pet is still present, you begin to grieve. You can wonder, "Is this the last time?" while you watch them sleep. After waking up, you can feel happy that they are still breathing, but you might feel guilty about feeling relieved.

To say goodbye for such a long time is emotionally draining. There may be brief periods of tranquility, but it may also leave questions unanswered. Is it possible that I waited for too long? Do I have enough to say? How terrified were they? The thoughts that you have are every day. It is from the exact origin of your love that they originate.

LOSS DUE TO FINANCIAL OR HOUSING CIRCUMSTANCES

Loss does not necessarily result in death. People are sometimes compelled to rehome their pets, resulting in their loss. The loss of a job, the inability to get housing, health problems, or the need to care for a pet may make it impossible to continue providing care for the animal, even if the attachment between you is strong.

Feelings of shame frequently accompany this grieving. Even though they made the most humane and responsible decision possible, people may feel they have disappointed their pets. Some people may have feelings of being judged by their family or friends. Having the knowledge that your pet is still alive but is no longer yours causes a persistent ache in your chest.

Rehoming can be a distressing experience for some people. Animals can be adopted by strangers or placed in shelters. The pain is compounded by the fact that one does not know. They may be missing you, that they are secure, and that they are experiencing feelings of abandonment. Grief is a genuine emotion. Support is warranted for it.

LOSS DUE TO DIVORCE, FAMILY CONFLICT, OR SEPARATION

It is not uncommon for the breakdown of a relationship to also result in the loss of a pet. In a custody dispute or a breakup, one person can keep the pet while the other is forced to move on. This might feel like the loss of a child, even in situations where the split is amicable. Sentiments of wrath, betrayal, or legal helplessness can complicate the sadness experienced.

In situations like these, sadness is caused by multiple layers of loss. In this way, the pet represents a life that is no longer present. People may experience feelings of helplessness, heartbreak, and being abandoned. Furthermore, because the animal is still alive, there may be pressure to "move on," even while the agony is very severe.

Even though this kind of loss is frequently disregarded, it can be as severe and long-lasting as any other kind.

WHO THIS BOOK IS FOR

Grief touches everyone differently. And when it comes to pet loss, there is no single profile of who is affected. This book was written with an open heart, knowing that the bond between humans and animals crosses every demographic, lifestyle, and circumstance.

CHILDREN

For many children, losing a pet is their first encounter with death. They may not understand the permanence of their feelings or how to express them. Some cry openly. Others become quiet, withdrawn, or even angry.

Grieving children need support that is honest and age-appropriate. They need space to ask questions—sometimes over and over. They need rituals and ways to remember, just like adults do. And most importantly, they need adults who validate their feelings instead of dismissing them.

This book offers guidance for supporting children during pet loss. Whether you're a parent, teacher, or caregiver, you'll find ways to help a child make sense of their emotions—and to heal alongside them.

SENIORS

For older adults, the loss of a pet can feel especially isolating. Many seniors live alone, and a pet might be their primary companion. Pets offer routine, purpose, and affection. When that presence disappears, the silence can be overwhelming.

Some may also fear judgment—being told they're "too old" to grieve so deeply. Others may worry about getting another pet and facing loss again. These feelings are complex and valid.

This book supports seniors navigating the unique emotional terrain of later-life pet loss. It affirms that their grief matters and that their bond is not just meaningful—but vital.

PEOPLE WITH DISABILITIES OR CHRONIC ILLNESS

For those managing long-term health conditions or disabilities, a pet may be more than a friend—they may be a support system. Service and emotional support animals provide safety, routine, and emotional grounding. Their loss can feel destabilizing.

Practical fears may also accompany the grief. Who will help me now? How will I cope without them? These questions are real. The loss is layered—not just emotional but functional.

This book holds space for that experience. It recognizes that pets are caregivers, too. And when a caregiver is lost, the grieving process must be met with care and compassion.

VETERINARIANS, VET TECHS, AND ANIMAL WORKERS

Those who work with animals are often surrounded by both life and death. They witness joy, pain, healing, and heartbreak—sometimes all in the same day. Over time, this emotional exposure can take a toll.

Veterinarians, rescue workers, shelter employees, and pet groomers may experience what's known as compassion fatigue. They may carry the weight of many losses, some deeply personal, others professional—but no less painful.

This book acknowledges their grief, too. It recognizes the emotional labor of working with animals and the need for healing spaces where that grief is honored instead of ignored.

YOU

Ultimately, this book is for you. Whether you're grieving the death of a pet, the loss of one through life's circumstances, or the fading memory of a companion from years past—your experience matters.

You don't need a label. You don't need permission. You need space to feel what you feel. And that's what this book aims to offer.

Reflections & Next Steps

- What kind of loss are you grieving? Was it sudden, expected, or shaped by circumstances beyond your control?
- Have you found yourself comparing your grief to someone else's? What would happen if you permitted yourself to feel full without comparison?
- What would you say if you could write a letter to someone who didn't understand your loss?
- What kind of support do you need most right now—and where might you find it?

PART II
MOVING THROUGH GRIEF

CHAPTER 4
FACING THE FIRST DAYS

It seemed like the bed was overly huge. There was an excessive amount of silence in the corridor. In the vicinity, there were no sounds of footsteps, a tail thumping against the floor, or soft breathing. There was no need to pour kibble, no leash waiting at the door, and no cause to step outside into the cold other than to feel the air and recall what it used to mean. Morning arrived, but there was no need whatsoever. The first few days after the death of a pet are like being placed into a world that appears to be the same, but it no longer feels like home.

These formative days are fragile, perplexing, and emotionally raw for the child. A feeling of emptiness or intolerability has taken hold of everything before automatic. There is a constant presence of reminders. The sound of nails striking tile is still something you anticipate hearing when you enter the kitchen. As a matter of routine, you grab the bag of treats. When you need to make room in bed for someone who is no longer present, you move over instinctually. These days, the feeling of sadness is at its most intense and palpable in a way that is difficult for language to convey adequately.

This adventure portion does not come with a booklet containing instructions. There is no way to prepare for the inevitable moment when love transforms into a memory. Nevertheless, awareness of what you might go through and what you can do can stabilize you during the storm.

EMOTIONAL SHOCK: WHEN EVERYTHING FEELS SURREAL

Grief can alter the passage of time. During the first few days, you could have a sense of confusion, as if your mind is unable to comprehend the fact that your pet has passed away fully. You can have a numbing sensation or an odd sense of serenity. Either you cry endlessly, or you don't cry at all. Specific individuals find themselves giggling out of the blue. To some people, it seems as though they are floating outside of their bodies and simply going through the motions. Any of these responses are typical.

The body protects the heart through the process of shock. By doing so, it lessens the intensity of the pain, allowing you to endure it. We do not have a timetable for how long it will continue. When you wake up, you might believe that it was a dream. You may accidentally pick up the leash or call out your pet's name. Inaccuracies like these are not failures. They are manifestations of the depth of your affection for them and the degree to which your life was intricately intertwined with theirs.

TANGIBLE TASKS IN AN INTANGIBLE TIME

Even in times of sorrow, the world continues to change. Some duties must be executed, judgments must be made, and choices appear insurmountable. There are a lot of folks who feel unprepared during these first few days. If your pet passes away at home, you might not know what steps to take next. You could still be required to make arrangements for aftercare services even if the death took place at a medical facility.

Here are some suggestions that are both compassionate and practical regarding what to anticipate:

- You can contact a veterinarian, a local animal hospital, or a pet aftercare agency if your pet passes away at home. You can discuss the options of transportation, cremation, or burial with them. For some mobile veterinary services, euthanasia and body removal can even be performed after the animal has passed away.

- Several clinics will provide you with the option of private or communal cremation, as well as urns, souvenirs, or paw prints if you decide to go through with euthanasia. Hold on to your time. There is no requirement that you arrive at every conclusion right away.

- Depending on the restrictions that are in place in your area, you might be able to bury your pet in a pet cemetery or on your land. In addition, you can select a private grave marker or a biodegradable casket.

- Finding solace in cherished mementos such as fur clippings, paw impressions, or favorite toys is possible. There is no need to feel compelled to conserve or dispose of anything immediately. Permit yourself to move at your own pace.

Handling these tasks can feel overwhelming, but they can offer a small sense of control when you feel powerless. Ask a trusted friend or family member to help coordinate calls or appointments. You deserve support as you walk through this.

WHEN GRIEF LIVES IN THE BODY

The mental and emotional burden of loss is not confined to the heart alone; it frequently manifests itself in the body as well. It is common to experience symptoms such as fatigue, appetite changes, headaches, chest tightness, and stomach trouble. Some individuals experience restlessness. Some people sleep for long periods. You might find yourself pacing with frantic energy or crying till you feel physically sore. Both of these things are possible.

Your body is processing someone or something monumental. Feeling fragile is quite normal. Even in the smallest of ways, make an effort to respect your bodily needs:

- Drink water. Grief is dehydrating.
- Eat when you can. Gentle, nourishing foods are best.

- Rest. Even if you can't sleep, allow yourself stillness.
- Move your body. A slow walk, stretching, or standing outside for fresh air can offer relief.

These actions aren't meant to "fix" grief. They're tools for survival. Think of them as ways to care for the part of you that is still alive and healing.

THE FIRST CONVERSATIONS: SHARING THE NEWS

Informing other people can be one of the most challenging aspects. Having the words spoken out loud brings the loss into focus. Some individuals avoid it entirely because they are not prepared to deal with the onslaught of sympathy or, even worse, indifference.

You are free to choose who you should tell, what you should say to them, and when you should tell them. Neither an immediate explanation nor an emotional performance is something that you owe to anyone. You can share at your speed.

If you decide to share something on social media, you are free to keep it straightforward or express everything in your heart. Sharing photographs, writing tributes, or encouraging others to share memories is frequently a source of solace for individuals. These seemingly insignificant acts of recollection have the potential to be highly therapeutic.

Make sure you are ready for a wide variety of types of reactions. A few people will express their deepest sympathies. People may make mistakes with their words or say something upsetting without intending to do so. The saying "You'll get another one" is designed to be comforting; nonetheless, it frequently fails to get the notion across. It is crucial to keep in mind that their discomfort is not a signal of your loss.

THE FIRST NIGHT WITHOUT THEM

On the first night after the death of a pet, there is a particular challenge that is not shared by any other. It is more difficult to hear. The absence is more noticeable. You tend to reach for your hands, which causes them to hurt. Your imagination may replay memories of their last moments or run through hypothetical situations. It could be challenging to fall asleep.

Gentleness is required for this night and the nights that will follow. Consider lighting a candle, wrapping yourself in the blanket they prefer, keeping a leash or collar close at hand, and putting together a letter. I am uttering their name out loud. Not only are these not rites of closure, but they are also bridges between the present and the past.

Bereavement does not require you to "let go" of something overnight. In reality, all you need is to allow yourself to feel.

FIRST AID FOR THE HEART: EMOTIONAL SELF-CARE

Try to befriend your grief in the days ahead rather than resist it. That doesn't mean wallowing. It means acknowledging your pain with kindness, not judgment.

Here are a few emotional "first aid" ideas:

- Create space for feelings. Whether it's crying, journaling, or simply staring at their photo, permit yourself to feel what you feel.
- Avoid self-judgment. There is no such thing as grieving "too much" or "too little." Grief is not a contest or a test. It's a process.
- Talk to someone who understands. A friend, therapist, support group, or online forum can help. Sometimes, just hearing "me too" makes all the difference.
- Speak to your pet. Tell them what you miss. Thank them. Say goodbye—again and again, if needed.

Remember, this is not about "moving on." It's about honoring what was lost and learning to carry it forward with love.

WHEN YOU DON'T KNOW WHAT TO DO WITH YOURSELF

In the past, routines were a source of comfort; now, they feel empty. These occasions, such as mealtime, walks, and nighttime rituals, become bitter reminders of the past. You may experience feelings of aimlessness, uncertainty, and disconnection. That is very typical.

If you want to fill the space, try using some soft structure. Every day, at the same time, you should prepare a cup of tea. A walk along the same path is recommended. Put on some music. Set a candle ablaze. Take a shower, write in your notebook, or make a phone call. Set one little activity.

Neither of these are distractions. The anchors are these. They bring to your attention the fact that time is continuously passing. There is still the possibility of healing. Although it has been changed, that life persists.

THE QUESTION THAT LINGERS: "WILL I EVER FEEL OKAY AGAIN?"

If you want a quick answer, the answer is yes; however, it won't be okay in the same way. Grief alters us forever. It works to restructure the heart. You will never forget the love you shared with your pet, but the absence of your pet will always be a part of your tale.

After some time has passed, the sharpness will become less pronounced. It will become a more subdued ache as time goes on. In the most unexpected of settings, joy will come back. Whenever you think about them, you will be able to grin. Their peculiarities will make you laugh out loud. You will not be able to forget them without snapping.

Although you may never "get over" this loss, you don't have to. With it, you will develop further.

REFLECTIONS & NEXT STEPS

- What part of your routine feels most painful without your pet? What made that moment special?
- How did you feel during the first night without them? If you could say something to them now, what would it be?
- What is one small ritual you could create in their honor—a candle, a walk, a journal?
- Write a message to your future self. What do you hope you've learned or healed six months from now?

CHAPTER 5
NAMING AND NAVIGATING EMOTIONS

During the early stages of mourning, there is a time when you find yourself caught between numbness and overwhelming feelings. When you suddenly find yourself laughing and then feeling guilty for laughing, or when you cry for no apparent reason. You may be feeling good one moment and completely falling apart the next. If you don't feel anything, you could start to question if there's something wrong with you. The emotional landscape of losing a pet is wild, unpredictable, and very human. This is the territory I am referring to.

There is a vast range of feelings that come along with grieving the loss of a beloved animal, many of which can appear to be in contradiction with one another or confused. You may feel terrible but also relieved. Feeling guilty while also angry. It was empty, but our memories still surrounded it. These are not incompatible ideas; instead, they are traveling companions on the path to recovery after loss. It is not about resolving your pain that you can comprehend and identify them. It is about making room for your experience to take place. Honoring the truth about what this relationship meant is the focus of this endeavor.

SADNESS AND THE WEIGHT OF ABSENCE

When it comes to grieving, sadness is frequently the most noticeable component. The agony that you feel in your chest as you walk by their bed that is empty. Tears that come out of nowhere and without notice. There is a deep yearning that comes over you when you understand that they are not going to return. There is more to this melancholy than simply missing them; it is also about mourning the person you were while they were in your life.

The feeling of sadness is persistent for some people. In the case of some individuals, it manifests itself in waves, initially intense and abrupt and then gradually diminishing. There is no shame in experiencing profound emotions. A measure of love is measured by sadness. Don't be afraid to cry. Remind yourself of the events. Your anguish is a holy thing.

GUILT: THE VOICE THAT QUESTIONS EVERYTHING

When a pet passes away, one of the most difficult feelings to experience is guilt. It asks queries in a low voice in the stillness. "Did I accomplish enough?" "Was it the opportunity to do so?" Did they get the sense that I loved them? The feeling of shame is familiar, regardless of whether your pet passed away suddenly or through euthanasia.

Sometimes, people feel guilty that they did not notice the symptoms sooner. In their final days, some people lament that they did not spend more time with their pets. Some people worry if their pet was harmed or if they should have taken a different course of action. When it comes to guilt, this voice can be unrelenting.

On the other hand, here is the fact: You had feelings for them. You gave it your all. It was your heart, not your ego, that guided your decision-making. Guilt is not evidence that you have failed; it is evidence of how much you cared about something. In addition, there are occasions when the required response is compassion rather than reprimand.

ANGER: THE UNSPOKEN GRIEF

Many individuals are reluctant to confess their anger, particularly when grieving. But that is true, and it is a valid argument. The veterinarian may cause you to feel upset. Regarding the sickness. At your own pace. The entire world. As a result of how unfair everything is, you could feel angry. Do you have a pet? Why at this time?

The feeling of helplessness is a common trigger for anger. It gives a voice to those who are helpless. As is the case with all feelings, it requires room. The following are examples of outbursts that are not considered childish: punching a pillow, going for a fast walk, ranting in the car, and writing an unfiltered journal entry. In other words, they are manifestations of a heart in pain.

If you want to feel rage, you should not suppress it. That won't be the case forever. However, putting up a fight against it can cause it to expand. Rather than repressing oneself, expression is the way to get freedom.

RELIEF: THE EMOTION THAT COMES WITH GUILT'S SHADOW

People rarely discuss the feeling of relief, but it is something that many people feel. When your pet's pain is finally relieved, it may be a sign of relief if they have been suffering from a prolonged sickness or decline. It is a relief to know that the decisions are now behind you. You can finally relax now, which is a relief.

Next, guilt makes its appearance. Does it mean I didn't love them enough if I get a sense of relief from them? No. Even in the same breath, one can experience both relief and love. It is not their departure that relieves you; it is the end of their indescribable anguish. When one is exhausted, when one is caring, or when one is anticipating something, it is a natural response. Even though you are feeling better, you are still permitted to grieve.

SHAME: THE HIDDEN LAYER OF PAIN

Unlike guilt, shame is not the same thing. Shame is a statement that states, "There is something wrong with me," in contrast to guilt, which says, "I did something wrong." Shame frequently manifests itself in the form of self-judgment following the death of a pet. Why am I in such a state of disrepair? "It was nothing more than a pet." "There are other people who are in a worse situation."

When people are silent, shame grows. It becomes more prevalent when sadness is disregarded or misinterpreted. When the people around you diminish the loss you have experienced, you may begin to question your feelings. However, here is the truth: there is absolutely nothing wrong with experiencing profound grief. There is absolutely nothing wrong with requiring some time. Grief is not a sign of weakness; rather, it is a mode of love.

Be honest with yourself. Bring up their name. Share your feelings of melancholy. When exposed to light, shame is unable to endure.

ANXIETY AND THE SEARCH FOR SAFETY

The feeling of being safe is thrown off by grief. Our routines are disrupted. There is no longer any emotional anchor. It is not uncommon to experience feelings of anxiety after the death of a pet, particularly if the animal served as a form of solace, stability, or support.

During this time, you might discover that you cannot concentrate, are hyperaware, and are restless. Some individuals suffer from panic attacks or insomnia. Some people experience terror without being able to explain why. There is a pattern to this anxiousness. It is your body's way of reacting to sudden changes and the loss of something.

A few examples of grounding activities are taking deep breaths, going for a stroll, holding a soothing object, talking to someone, or writing. Reassure yourself in the same way that you would reassure a friend: "You are safe. You are experiencing grief. This sensation is only temporary."

Emptiness and Numbness

Some days, the emotions are loud. Other days, there is nothing. Just a quiet blankness. A numbness that sits in your body like fog. You may feel like you're watching your life from outside yourself. This detachment is common.

Numbness is the nervous system's way of protecting you from emotional overload. It doesn't mean you don't care. It means your system is conserving energy. Be patient. The feelings will return—but only when you're ready to hold them again.

Love: The Emotion Beneath Them All

Each sense of sorrow has its origins in love. All the emotions, including the tears, anger, guilt, and desire, point back to one fundamental truth: you had genuine affection for your pet. They had feelings for you.

The love that you feel does not vanish. Just like that, it transforms. Time transforms it into a memory, a legacy, and a ritual. You still pause when you hear their favorite music, which lives on in the photographs you take, your fantasies, and the way. You have it within you.

Permit yourself to go back to that love whenever the feelings get overwhelming. Take a deep breath in. Rely on it to hold you.

Making Room for Every Emotion

You do not have to explain your emotions. You don't have to justify how long it's been or how "bad" it feels. You don't have to sort through them perfectly or understand them immediately. You have to let them be.

Try this: Name what you feel, even if it's uncomfortable. Say it aloud. "I feel guilt." "I feel sadness." "I feel empty." Naming softens the sharp edges. It turns chaos into something that can be held.

And then remind yourself: "This is normal. This is part of grief. I don't have to fix it. I have to feel it."

Reflections & Next Steps

- What emotion has surprised you most during this grieving process? How has it shown up?
- Are you judging any of your feelings right now? What would it sound like to respond with compassion instead?
- Write down three emotions you've experienced since your pet's passing. Then write a letter from your pet to you, responding to each one with love.
- When you feel overwhelmed, what brings you comfort? Can you create a ritual to return to that feeling?

CHAPTER 6
LETTING GO OF GUILT

Slowly, like a whisper in the back of my mind, the guilt began to take hold. Next, the volume increased. Every memory was rewritten, conversations were rewritten, and decisions were called into question. What would have happened if I had discovered it earlier? "Why did I not remain home on that particular day?" "Did they have any idea how crazy I was about them?"

In many cases, grief and guilt are inseparable companions, particularly when a cherished pet has passed away. Guilt can creep in even when there is no mistake, no delay, and no misstep. It clings to moments that merit sympathy rather than punishment and asks questions that would be impossible to answer.

Doing something wrong is not necessarily the cause of guilt. Your heart is still striving to make sense of the loss, which says a lot about how strongly you loved the person. Rather than judging or erasing such feelings, this chapter provides a secure environment to unpack and gently release them, one breath at a time.

THE NATURE OF GUILT IN PET LOSS

Guilt after pet loss is often more intense than people expect. It can feel all-consuming, especially if the loss involves decision-making, as with euthanasia. The "what-ifs" spiral easily:

- "What if I had taken them to the vet sooner?"
- "What if I hadn't gone on that trip?"

- "What if I had chosen differently?"

These thoughts arise because your heart is still loving, searching for a way to make the pain sense. Guilt gives the illusion of control. It tricks you into thinking that you could have saved them if you had done something differently. But loss is not a math problem. Love does not prevent death.

In truth, guilt is often a mask for grief. It's what happens when love meets powerlessness. You loved them—and you couldn't stop the end. That helplessness is excruciating—guilt steps in to fill the space.

The Guilt of Euthanasia

No decision weighs heavier than choosing to end a beloved pet's life. Even when the evidence is clear—pain, decline, suffering—the heart doesn't want to say goodbye. And afterward, many people carry a deep, aching guilt.

You may wonder:

- "Did I give up too soon?"
- "Did they understand what was happening?"
- "Did I fail them when they needed me most?"

These are natural, human questions. They come from a place of love. But here's what matters most: you made that decision not out of selfishness but compassion. You chose peace over prolonged pain. That is not betrayal. That is mercy.

One of the most powerful truths about euthanasia is this: it is an act of love that puts your pet's comfort above your heartbreak. It is selfless. It is brave. And it is devastating. You shouldn't have to carry that weight alone.

When You Blame Yourself for Missing the Signs

Sometimes, the source of guilt is not the conclusion but the events that occurred before it. The day that you became aware that they were not eating. You choose to disregard the cough. This behavior appeared peculiar but was not taken seriously. Based on hindsight, everything seems to be a sign. Grief, on the other hand, tends to rewrite memories with the keen pen of hindsight.

Pets are experts at concealing their discomfort. They instinctively conceal symptoms. Even owners who are extremely vigilant and attentive are prone to missing signs. It does not mean that you are a careless person. It is what makes you human.

You arrived in the manner that you were able to do so. Every day, you showed concern. It is impossible to overcome a lifetime of love with a missed clue.

THE GUILT OF ABSENCE

Specific individuals were absent during the last minutes. Their absence was due to work, travel, or other life situations. The absence of that person becomes a significant burden. It turned out that the final farewell did not go as they had anticipated. Either did not take place at all.

When you are absent, punishing yourself for your absence is simple. But guilt cannot erase the fact that you had no control over the situation. Your pet would have understood if they had been aware of the explanations you gave them. They had known your affection for innumerable moments before that particular day. They could sense it in how you held them, played with them, fed them, and gave them protection.

It is more than just a minute to be present. It encompasses the entirety of the life that you both shared.

RITUALS FOR RELEASING GUILT

Guilt doesn't vanish by force. It softens with acknowledgment, ritual, and time. These practices may help you gently release what you've been carrying:

1. Write a Letter to Your Pet

Pour everything onto the page. Say what you wish you'd done. Ask what you need to ask. Say sorry if you must—but also say thank you. Then, write a reply from your pet. Imagine their voice. What would they say to comfort you? To forgive you? To remind you of what you meant to them?

2. Speak Aloud What You've Been Holding

Find a quiet space. Light a candle. Say the words out loud. "I'm sorry." "I miss you." "I did my best." Naming your guilt is a powerful way to loosen its grip.

3. Create a Guilt-Release Ritual

Write your guilt on slips of paper and burn them safely. Bury them. Toss them into water. Do something physical to mark the release. Let the action reflect the intention: to forgive yourself.

4. Practice a Guided Meditation or Visualization

There are meditations explicitly designed for releasing guilt and grief. Picture your pet healthy, joyful, free. Let them approach you. Let them forgive you. Let them say goodbye.

Affirmations to Gently Reframe Your Guilt

Sometimes, we need new words to speak into the silence of guilt. These affirmations are not meant to erase your feelings but to offer a different way of seeing them:

- "I did the best I could with the knowledge I had."
- "My pet knew love every single day."
- "I made choices with care, not cruelty."
- "Guilt is a sign of love, not failure."
- "I forgive myself for being human."

Say them aloud. Write them down. Carry them with you. Let them be your new inner voice.

WHEN FORGIVENESS FEELS IMPOSSIBLE

Some guilt is stubborn. It sticks around no matter how often you try to let it go. If this is true for you, know that healing isn't linear. Forgiveness is not a switch you flip—it's a process.

You may need to talk to someone: a therapist, a grief counselor, or a pet loss support group. You may need time to revisit memories with more tenderness and less judgment. You may need to return to your rituals again and again.

That's okay. Forgiveness isn't something you give yourself once. It's something you practice slowly, like rebuilding trust with a hurting part of yourself.

YOUR PET WOULDN'T WANT YOU TO SUFFER

This is perhaps the most essential truth: If your pet could see your pain, they would want you to be free of it. They wouldn't want you to carry shame or guilt. They would nudge your hand, curl beside you, lick your tears.

They loved you unconditionally. They forgave instantly. Their heart was not bound by regret—only love.

Let their love be your permission to begin letting go.

REFLECTIONS & NEXT STEPS

- What are the words guilt keeps repeating to you? Write them down. Then respond with love.
- If your pet could speak to you now, what would they say about how you treat yourself?
- Try one guilt-release ritual this week, even if it's simple—Journal how it made you feel.
- Write a forgiveness statement. Begin with, "Today, I choose to begin forgiving myself for..."

CHAPTER 7
THE TRUTH ABOUT
THE 5 STAGES

At the very instant when the tears began to fall, you had the idea, "This must be depression." When you felt angry at the veterinarian, yourself, or the world, you believed this was also a part of the growing process. As you finally found yourself laughing at a memory, you wondered, "Is this acceptance?" Is it possible that I am "through" the stages?

Grief does not adhere to a predetermined pattern. As a result of whatever they have read, heard, or been told in the past, many individuals enter it believing it should. Denial, anger, bargaining, sadness, and acceptance comprise the "five stages" model of grieving, which has now grown so prevalent that it is viewed like a map. However, grief, especially over a pet, does not develop this way.

Anger can be the first emotion that comes to your mind. Alternatively, you might completely avoid denial. You may believe you're in all five stages at the same time. You are free to return any of them indefinitely. In no way is this a failure. This is the true nature of grief: it is unpredictable, cyclical, and entirely human.

WHERE THE FIVE STAGES CAME FROM

Elisabeth Kubler-Ross, a psychiatrist, established the concept of the five stages of grief in the late 1960s. The purpose of this concept was to provide a means of describing the emotional reactions of terminally ill patients who were confronting their mortality. Subsequently, the model was utilized more comprehensively to encompass all types of loss, including bereavement. However, even though Kubler-Ross never intended for the stages to be construed as linear or prescriptive, this is how they were frequently understood.

People started treating their grief as if it were a ladder. That which can be climbed. Something that has a culminating point. Unrealistic expectations were established due to this, particularly for those individuals whose grief did not follow that path.

There is no set routine for grieving the loss of a cherished pet. Moving through a series of feelings and emerging "healed" on the other side is not the point of this. Learning to live with a new shape in your heart is the focus of this lesson. one that expresses both the affection and the loss that has occurred.

GRIEF IS NOT LINEAR

When it comes to grieving, there is no endpoint. To achieve peace, you must not finish all of the phases. There is no way to move from melancholy to acceptance, just like you can't mark items off a list.

One day, you might feel at peace, yet you might fall apart the next day. It is possible that you will be happy at breakfast but will be crying by lunch. You may believe that you are "doing better" and then allow the sound of their tags jingling in a recollection to bring you down. It is not a case of going backward. Not a failure, this is not. Grief is how it is.

It is like waves that move grief, just like the seasons. That is, swirls. There is a recirculation, a change in shape, a silent arrival, and a booming sound of impact. You will experience days when you feel you are far away from the anguish, and there will be days when you are right back in the middle of it. This does not mean that you are unable to move forward. It is a sign that your love is still operating.

THE STAGE OF DENIAL—OR THE GIFT OF NUMBNESS

It's not always the case that denial is disbelief. Every once in a while, it's emotional remoteness. A feeling of numbness that penetrates your body and creates a distance between you and the full impact of what has occurred.

If you wake up, you might temporarily forget they are no longer there. If you are not fully present, you may get the impression that you are simply going through the motions of your day, such as eating yourself and going about your business. This is your mind guarding your heart from possible harm. As a result, you will have more time to adjust to the new reality.

No, denial is not an indication that one is disconnected. It is a subtle buffer that enables the grieving process to unfold gradually.

THE STAGE OF ANGER— OR THE NEED FOR JUSTICE AND CONTROL

When someone is grieving, anger frequently receives a negative reputation. It is perceived by many as being illogical or unpleasant. On the other hand, rage is a normal reaction to a loss. This voice makes the statement, "This isn't fair." What caused this to take place? Why is it now?

You can feel angry at the veterinarian, fate, or other people who don't comprehend what you're going through. Possibly, you feel furious at yourself regarding your pet and the entire planet for continuing to exist without them.

Nothing is wrong with this rage. Fixing it is not an issue at all. It is a feeling that I want to be observed by others. It frequently depicts the love of searching for a place to settle down. Make it possible for yourself to express it through movement, writing, or words. When it is allowed to talk, it will become more pliable.

The Stage of Bargaining— Or the Echoes of "What If"

Bargaining is not always about making deals with the universe. It often shows up as looping thoughts:

- "What if I had noticed sooner?"
- "What if I'd taken them to a different vet?"
- "What if I'd canceled that trip?"

These questions are an attempt to rewrite the ending. To find a way to make it hurt less. But grief has no loopholes. And there's no version of the story that would make saying goodbye feel easy.

Bargaining is a mind trying to comfort a broken heart. It's a natural part of loss—but not one that brings answers. The only response it truly needs is compassion.

The Stage of Depression— Or the Depth of Missing

During this period, the burden of grief is at its greatest. The energy level lowers. The melancholy continues to linger. You get a sense of calmness that permeates your entire framework.

The act of getting out of bed could be difficult for you. Things you used to enjoy may no longer hold your interest. One can ponder whether or not this burden will ever be lifted. This is the complete spectrum of mourning. Also, there is no need to speed through it.

The loss of a pet can bring about a profound and secluded sorrow that others might not recognize or comprehend. However, that is a legitimate argument. This is authorized. In addition, you are not the only one who feels this way.

There are times when this depression does not require repairing; instead, it requires holding. Exercise kindness toward yourself. Allow the melancholy to move. It is going to change.

THE STAGE OF ACCEPTANCE— OR THE BEGINNING OF CARRYING IT DIFFERENTLY

Many people have the wrong idea about acceptance. Not forgetting is not the same thing. It does not mean that you are okay with what happened. It is not synonymous with "moving on."

It entails coming to terms with the fact that your pet has passed away while recognizing that the love you had for them will continue to exist. In other words, it is discovering ways to deal with the loss without allowing it to crush you. That means that looking at a photograph makes you smile more than cry. It involves creating a life in which they continue to be a part of your narrative, even when absent.

Acceptance is not a destination. One can say that it is a return to oneself.

GRIEF DOESN'T NEED STAGES— IT NEEDS SPACE

Rather than trying to move through stages, what if you gave yourself space to feel? What if you let grief be what it is—a sacred, personal, unpredictable process?

Your grief might not look like anyone else's. That doesn't make it wrong. It makes it yours.

Some days, you may need to talk. On other days, you may need silence. Some days will feel manageable. Others may feel unbearable. But every feeling is part of healing.

You're not behind. You're not doing it wrong. You are grieving—and that, in itself, is enough.

A New Metaphor: Grief as Weather

If the stages feel too rigid, try thinking of grief as weather. It changes daily. Sometimes hourly. There are sunny moments, sudden storms, quiet drizzles, and unexpected downpours.

You don't control the weather. You learn to carry an umbrella. To seek shelter when needed. To let it pass. You don't judge yourself for rain. You prepare for it. You wait it out. You find beauty even in the clouds.

Grief is the same. Let it move. Let it speak. And trust that the sun will return.

REFLECTIONS & NEXT STEPS

- Have you found yourself trying to "follow" the five stages? What expectations have you placed on your grief?
- What metaphor speaks more clearly to your experience than stages— weather, waves, spirals, something else?
- Write down a moment this week when grief surprised you. What did it teach you?
- If you feel "stuck" in a particular emotion, what would it feel like to make space for it instead of trying to move past it?

PART III
HONORING AND MEMORIALIZING

CHAPTER 8
HEALING RITUALS
AND TRIBUTES

The hook that holds the leash is still located near the entrance. Even though you know they will not come running when it jingles, you cannot take it down. Not at this time. Perhaps not at any point in time. Rather than being a symbol of regularity, it is now a symbol of affection. The walks, the experiences, and the peaceful moments that were shared. It is a repository of memories your heart is unprepared to let go of.

THAT'S THE POWER OF RITUAL.

The world doesn't pause when a pet dies—no funerals with hymns or eulogies. Often, you're expected to return to life as if nothing changed. But everything has changed. And your heart still needs a way to mark the loss, honor the love, and remember.

Rituals and tributes are not about letting go. They're about holding on in a way that brings comfort. They shape your grief, help you express what words can't, and offer healing through intention. They remind you that love didn't die when your pet did—it simply changed form.

WHY RITUALS MATTER IN PET GRIEF

Rituals are acts of love made visible. In human grief, we often have culturally recognized practices—funerals, memorials, obituaries. But pet grief tends to exist in private. And yet, the bond with a pet can be just as deep, the pain just as raw.

When grief has no outlet, it becomes stagnant. Rituals allow motion. They don't erase pain, but they help it move. They provide meaning, structure, and a way to continue the relationship with your pet in a new way.

You don't need candles or ceremonies (though you can have them). A ritual can be as small as whispering their name into your pillow, lighting incense, or sitting in their favorite spot each evening. What matters is the intention behind the act. That's where the healing lives.

CREATING A MEMORIAL AT HOME

Many people find comfort in setting up a home tribute. It can be a framed photo on a shelf or an elaborate display with candles, a collar, and favorite toys. This space becomes sacred—sit with your memories, speak your love, and feel close.

Consider including:

- A framed photo or pawprint
- Their collar, tags, or a favorite toy
- A handwritten letter or journal entry
- A candle you light at the same time each day
- Flowers, stones, or items from nature
- A small bowl of water as a symbol of peace

You don't need permission to create this space. It's yours. It can be temporary or permanent. Private or shared. Add to it as you feel moved. Let it grow with your healing.

PLANNING A GOODBYE CEREMONY

Holding a farewell ceremony is a powerful way to mark the transition from life to memory. This doesn't need to be formal. It doesn't need to involve others. It just needs to reflect your bond.

Some ideas for a meaningful ceremony:

- Read a letter aloud to your pet
- Play a song that reminds you of them
- Share stories with loved ones
- Scatter flower petals, release a balloon, or plant a tree
- Hold the ceremony at their favorite place—under a tree, by the beach, in the backyard
- Include other pets, giving them space to say goodbye too

Ceremonies give structure to sorrow. They offer a beginning, middle, and end to the moment, not the love. The love continues.

LIGHTING CANDLES AND SETTING REMEMBRANCE RITUALS

Light has long been used as a symbol of hope and memory. Lighting a candle in your pet's honor can be a simple, powerful practice. It says, "I remember." It says, "Your light is still with me."

Consider lighting a candle:

- On the day of their passing
- Each night for a week
- On their birthday or adoption day
- During the holidays
- Whenever you miss them deeply

Pair the candle with a quiet reflection, a photo, or a spoken message. Over time, this ritual becomes an anchor—something steady to return to in waves of grief.

VIRTUAL TRIBUTES AND ONLINE MEMORIALS

In today's digital world, remembering doesn't have to be confined to physical space. Many people create online memorials or social media posts to honor their pets. These tributes invite the community, encourage connection, and allow others to say, "I see your love."

Some ideas:

- Create a photo slideshow with your pet's favorite moments
- Write a post sharing their story, quirks, and what they meant to you
- Use a hashtag to collect memories from others who knew them
- Join an online pet memorial site and light a digital candle

These virtual spaces can become places of comfort—returning to old posts, rereading comments, and remembering that your grief is shared, not solitary.

ANNIVERSARY REMEMBRANCE DAYS

Specific dates will return with weight as time passes: the day you brought them home, the day you said goodbye, and the season when they always seemed happiest. These anniversaries can bring fresh grief and an opportunity to honor the bond.

Ways to mark a remembrance day:

- Visit their favorite place
- Donate to an animal shelter in their name
- Write a new journal entry or poem
- Please light a candle or set flowers near their photo
- Cook a meal they would've begged for and savor the memory

Grief doesn't observe a calendar. But honoring these dates can transform sorrow into ritual and pain into love.

INCLUDING OTHERS IN TRIBUTE

Sometimes, grief feels less heavy when shared. Including loved ones in memorial acts can bring connection and healing. Whether it's family, friends, or neighbors who knew your pet, inviting others to remember with you can lighten the emotional load.

Ideas to involve others:

- Ask friends to send their favorite memories or photos
- Hold a virtual gathering to share stories
- Include children in a creative remembrance project
- Please invite others to light candles with you in their own homes, at the same time

Even if your pet was shy or didn't know many people, you are part of a community—and your grief deserves to be witnessed.

INCORPORATING SPIRITUAL OR CULTURAL PRACTICES

For some, healing comes through spiritual traditions. Whether you practice a faith or follow your rituals, including spiritual elements in your tribute is okay.

You might:

- Say a prayer or blessing over their resting place
- Use incense, bells, or sacred music
- Consult religious leaders or spiritual advisors for guidance
- Perform a ritual based on cultural tradition (such as the Day of the Dead)
- Journal about where you believe your pet's spirit has gone

Belief, whatever its form, can offer comfort. Trust your instincts. If a practice brings peace, it's worth exploring.

When It Feels Too Hard to Create a Ritual

Sometimes, grief is so raw that creating a tribute feels overwhelming. That's okay. You don't have to "do something" to prove your love. Sometimes, the greatest act of remembrance is simply sitting with the ache and letting it be.

If rituals feel too much, start small:

- Whisper their name in the morning
- Touch their collar gently
- Breathe and say, "You are still with me."

Healing doesn't need to be big to be real. It needs only to be honest.

Letting the Rituals Evolve Over Time

As your grief softens, your rituals may change. What once brought tears may someday bring peace. You might add to your memorial. You might move it. You might feel ready to close one chapter and open another. This is not forgotten. It's growing.

Rituals are not frozen in time. They move with your heart.

REFLECTIONS & NEXT STEPS

- What object, space, or action brings you closest to your pet's memory? How might that become part of a tribute?
- What would it look like if you could plan a simple ceremony in their honor? What words would you say?
- Light a candle tonight. Speak their name. Let yourself remember.
- Consider setting a future remembrance day—on their birthday, adoption date, or a meaningful season. How would you like to mark it?

CHAPTER 9
LEGACY PROJECTS

O n top of the bookcase, there was an antique collar that was sitting next to a small photograph that was framed. At first sight, it appeared to be nothing more than a collection of mementos. But for the guy who put it there, it was the most crucial thing in the world. It was the sound of complete confidence. It's a metaphor for a thousand different walks. A gentle reminder that love, even when it is not visible, continues to reverberate in the current moment. That collar was not gathering dust at any point. In doing so, it was preserving a memory.

The legacy projects are responsible for this. They ensure that the love you had for your pet is carried on, not as a means of forgetting but rather as a means of transforming your sadness into something meaningful. These endeavors are not about "getting over" the loss that has occurred. It's about allowing the love to continue to blossom after the parting is over.

To leave a legacy, grandeur is not necessary. It may be a private, limited, and discreet affair. It may serve a charity or creative purpose. A journal or a memorial garden could be the starting point for this endeavor. Either it will involve other people or remain solely between you and your pet. Most importantly, what is important is the aim, which is to commemorate their presence and to continue the story that you shared.

THE HEALING POWER OF CREATION

It is possible for everything to feel broken after a loss. There is a difference in the movement of time. The purpose could appear to be far away. On the other hand, creating anything in your pet's memory helps bring some order to chaotic situations. It provides a destination for your heart to go.

Projects that leave a legacy might serve as a connection between sadness and significance. The ability to take your sorrow, memories, and love and shape them into something that will last is made possible by them. Something wonderful. Something indicating that they were important. They continue to do so.

It is common for grief to feel helpless. Giving you back a sense of agency is making something, whether writing, building, contributing, or planting. You are not making an effort to alleviate the suffering. You're figuring out how to continue living with it.

Journals and Memory Books

One of the most accessible and profound legacy projects is creating a memory book. This could be a photo album, a scrapbook, or a handwritten journal that tells the story of your life together.

You might include:

- Your pet's baby photos, adoption day snapshots, or milestone moments
- Notes about their personality, quirks, and favorite things
- Stories of funny or meaningful experiences
- Letters you've written to them, or ones they might write to you
- Drawings, poems, or even paw prints pressed onto a page

A memory book gives form to the intangible. It allows you to see your pet's story, page by page, even as time progresses. And when grief feels heavy, flipping through those pages becomes a way to return to them—not in sadness, but in gratitude.

Social Media Tributes
and Digital Legacies

For many, their pets were part of their online world. Photos were posted, birthdays celebrated, and stories shared. When they pass, social media can become a space not only for mourning—but for legacy.

You might:

- Create a dedicated post to celebrate their life
- Start a memorial hashtag where others can add their memories
- Build a private or public digital album with friends and family
- Write a eulogy or obituary to share what they meant to you
- Record a video montage or slideshow and post it with music and reflections

Digital legacy allows others to witness your bond. It can spark conversations, encourage connection, and offer you ongoing support. It reminds you that your grief is not invisible—and neither was their life.

Donating in Their Name

Transforming grief into generosity can be a powerful act of healing. Donating to an animal shelter, rescue organization, or veterinary clinic in your pet's name keeps their spirit alive in the lives of other animals.

You don't have to give large sums. Even small gestures matter:

- Sponsor an adoption fee for a senior animal
- Purchase blankets, toys, or food for a local shelter
- Host a birthday fundraiser for your pet's "gotcha day" anniversary
- Donate books to a children's library about pet care and love
- Provide pet food to a family in need through a local pantry

These acts don't erase the pain—but they plant something new in the soil of your loss. They say: "This love didn't end—it grew."

Volunteering as a Tribute

Some people find healing by putting their hands to work. Volunteering at an animal shelter, rescue center, wildlife rehab, or pet therapy program can feel like a living tribute to the pet you lost. It's not about replacing them. It's about honoring what they inspired in you.

Your pet taught you love, patience, and care. Sharing those gifts with needy animals helps your grief become a legacy of compassion.

If volunteering with animals feels too hard at first, you might begin by:

- Helping with administrative tasks or fundraising for a shelter
- Supporting pet loss support groups as a listener
- Offering transportation for foster or rescue efforts
- Creating care packages for pets and their people in crisis

You're not filling the hole in your heart. You're using the love that remains to comfort others.

Gardens and Nature Memorials

Nature has a way of holding grief without words. Planting something in your pet's honor can be a symbolic gesture. Flowers, shrubs, trees—even herbs—can become living reminders of the love you shared.

Consider:

- Planting their favorite spot with flowers
- Creating a "remembrance garden" with steppingstones, wind chimes, or a small bench
- Placing a stone or statue in a peaceful outdoor space
- Adding a bird feeder to a window, they always watched from
- Using their ashes in a biodegradable urn designed to nourish a plant

Tending to something that grows—even as you grieve—offers a gentle reminder that love continues to bloom, even in sorrow.

PERSONAL KEEPSAKES AND CREATIVE TRIBUTES

Sometimes, healing happens through the hands. Creating something tactile—a piece of art, a handmade keepsake, a craft project—can be a meaningful way to process your grief.

You might try:

- Making jewelry with their name, birthstone, or ashes in a locket
- Designing a keychain from their tags
- Crafting a memory box with their collar, toys, and photos
- Painting a portrait or a favorite scene
- Writing a song or poem in their honor
- Sewing a small pillow or quilt from a blanket they loved

These aren't just crafts. They're containers of memory. Holding them can bring comfort during dark days and become heirlooms of the love you shared.

LIVING BY THEIR LEGACY

Sometimes, the most profound tribute is how you live. The choices you make. The values you carry forward. Ask yourself: What would they want for me now?

Perhaps they'd want you to rest more. Laugh more. Go on that walk you always skipped. Maybe they'd like you to open your heart again—not to forget them, but to love more because of them.

Living by their legacy could mean:

- Adopting another pet when you're ready—not to replace, but to expand your heart
- Continuing their routines in a new way: morning walks, sunset reflections, quiet cuddle time

- Being an advocate for animal welfare, education, or kindness
- Carrying their name forward in your life, your writing, or your work
- Becoming the person you were when they looked at you with love

Grief will soften over time, but their influence won't. Let their spirit shape who you become.

WHAT WOULD THEY WANT YOU TO DO?

One of the most powerful reflections after loss is this: What would they want me to do now?

Not as pressure—but as comfort. As purpose.

Would they want you to cry? Of course. But they'd also want you to eat, rest, and care for yourself. They'd like you to remember the joy. To laugh at their antics. To feel their presence in the little things.

Ask that question when the pain feels directionless. Let it guide you—not toward forgetting, but toward intentional healing.

Reflections & Next Steps

- What project, no matter how small, feels like a meaningful way to honor your pet's memory?
- If your pet could see your tribute, what would they think? Joy? Pride? Peace?
- Is there a way to use your grief to comfort someone else—or another animal in need?
- Write down one action you can take this week, however small, to continue their story in a visible, loving way.

CHAPTER 10
INVOLVING OTHERS
IN THE HEALING

Grief is often described as a solitary journey. And in many ways, it is. There is no one else who can fully comprehend the form that your loss has taken or the extent to which it hurts. However, healing does not have to take place in a solitary setting. The method by which the participation of other people can alter one's sorrow, whether those others share your grief or see it. It creates space for connection, understanding, and even consolation when the world seems meaningless.

It is simple to feel invisible after a much-loved pet's death. Although people may have good intentions, they frequently fail to comprehend. Even if they are communicated with the best intentions, phrases such as "you'll get another" or "they had a good life" might be perceived as dismissive. You may withdraw from others if you are unsure who to talk to or how much information to disclose.

However, healing never takes place in complete silence. You open the door to shared memories when you let other people participate in your grief process. This could be a kid, a partner, a friend, or even someone who shares your love for pets. At the same time that you help demolish the stigma associated with pet loss, you also permit people to grieve honestly.

EXPLAINING DEATH TO CHILDREN

Children frequently form their first profound emotional connection with their pets, which also happens to be their first genuine experience with death. It is possible to experience confusion and pain when one loses a furry, feathery, or scaled buddy. It is only natural for a caretaker to desire to protect their loved one from experiencing agony. On the other hand, integrity, when conveyed with affection, strengthens resiliency and emotional intelligence.

Children do not require flawless explanations; instead, they need presence. They must have a space to ask questions, repeat themselves, cry unexpectedly, and find satisfaction in your consistency.

Approaches that are helpful while communicating with children:

- Use clear, honest language. Avoid euphemisms like "went to sleep" or "ran away," which can create fear or confusion. Instead, say, "They died. That means their body stopped working, and they're not returning."
- Answer only what they ask. Let their curiosity guide the conversation. You don't need to explain everything at once.
- Validate their emotions. If they're angry, withdrawn, tearful, or silent—that's okay. Say things like, "It's okay to miss them," or "I feel sad too."
- Offer comfort through rituals. Drawing pictures, making a small memorial, lighting a candle, or reading a story about pet loss can help children process their feelings in age-appropriate ways.

Children are capable of deep empathy. Being honest and present allows them to navigate loss with trust and safety—skills that will serve them for life.

HELPING A PARTNER GRIEVE— OR GRIEVING DIFFERENTLY TOGETHER

The pet was "ours," not just "mine, " in many families or households." However, even shared pets experience this through individual bonds. One partner may feel grief more intensely or express it more openly than the other. One might need quiet; the other might need conversation. These differences can create tension—or they can create opportunities for deeper connection.

Here's how to support one another during joint grief:

- Communicate needs. Say, "I'd love to talk about them—would that be okay?" or "I need some time alone today." Being clear helps avoid misunderstandings.
- Respect grieving styles. One of you might find comfort in photos and stories; the other might need time before facing reminders. Neither is wrong.
- Share memories. Rewatch a favorite video, reminisce about a funny moment, or walk to a place you used to go with your pet.
- Create a joint ritual. Light a candle each evening. Visit their resting place together. These shared actions build closeness.

When approached with patience, compassion, and curiosity, grief can bring couples closer. It can also uncover old wounds or communication habits. This is a tender time—be gentle with each other.

INCLUDING OTHER PETS IN THE GRIEVING PROCESS

In multi-pet households, grief doesn't only affect humans. Surviving animals often sense the absence. They notice when routines change, when a familiar scent is gone, and when the household energy shifts.

Some animals show signs of grief—searching for their companion, refusing food, becoming anxious or withdrawn. Others may seem unaffected, but that doesn't mean they don't notice. Animals often process loss in their instinctive ways.

Ways to support grieving pets:

- Maintain routine. Structure helps animals feel safe. Keep feeding, walking, and play times consistent.

- Give extra affection. You're grieving together. Offering more touch, attention, and reassurance helps you both.
- Let them say goodbye. If possible, allow pets to see the body or be present during euthanasia. This can help reduce confusion.
- Watch for behavioral changes. Loss can affect appetite, sleep, and energy. Consult your vet if the behaviors persist.

Your bond with your surviving pet may deepen during this time. They become a bridge between what was and what still is. Let them be part of your healing.

When Friends or Family Don't Understand

Not everyone understands pet grief. You may encounter well-meaning people who unintentionally hurt you with words like:

- "It was just a dog."
- "You can always get another."
- "At least it wasn't a person."

These responses often come from discomfort, not malice. Some people haven't formed deep bonds with animals. Others are afraid of grief and don't know how to sit with it. Still, that doesn't mean you must tolerate dismissiveness.

Helpful ways to respond:

- "They were family to me. I miss them."
- "I appreciate your words, but I need someone to listen most right now."
- "This loss is tough, and I'd love your support."

You don't need to defend your grief. But you have the right to seek out people who make space for it—those who listen without judgment, remember your pet's name, and ask how you are doing weeks later.

FINDING OR CREATING A GRIEF SUPPORT CIRCLE

Sometimes, the best healing happens with people who've been there. Pet loss support groups—online or in person—can be incredibly comforting. Sharing stories, tears, and memories with others who "get it" reminds you that your grief is shared, not solitary.

These spaces offer:

- Nonjudgmental listening
- Practical advice for navigating emotions
- Validation of your experience
- Opportunities for Memorial Rituals
- Lasting friendships based on a shared love for animals

If you can't find a group near you, consider starting one. Even a monthly meetup at a coffee shop or a private Facebook group can become a sanctuary for others who feel isolated by their loss.

WHEN YOU FEEL LIKE YOU NEED TO HIDE YOUR GRIEF

Many people feel pressure to "be strong," "move on," or "not make a fuss" about losing a pet. This pressure can be extreme in workplaces, communities that don't value pets as family, or among peers who've never had animals.

This invisibility can compound grief. It adds a layer of shame to sorrow. You may catch yourself hiding tears or pretending you're okay before you're ready.

But your grief deserves space. You don't need anyone's permission to mourn. You don't need to apologize for your heart.

Suppose you can speak openly about your loss to someone you trust. Use your voice. Share a story. Say their name. Whenever you talk about your pet with love, you honor their life and allow someone else to do the same.

Helping Others Understand How to Support You

Sometimes, people want to help but don't know how. You can guide them gently. You might say:

- "It helps when you ask about them."
- "I'd love it if you looked at a picture with me."
- "I don't need advice—I just need someone to listen."

When someone offers a kind gesture—bringing over flowers, checking in, texting a memory—let them know it matters. Even the smallest act of kindness can carry enormous weight during grief.

And if someone disappoints you, try to hold space for their limitations while protecting your heart. Not everyone knows how to show up. But some will surprise you in beautiful ways.

Making Space for Joy Again— with Others

As time passes, laughter will return. So will joy. It may feel strange at first— like you're betraying your grief or forgetting your pet. But joy is not betrayal. It's a sign of healing.

Involving others in joy—visiting a dog park together, sharing old videos, adopting another animal when you're ready—can feel like a bridge between what was and what's becoming.

Let joy come when it wants to. Let others walk with you into it. Grief and joy can—and often do—coexist.

Reflections & Next Steps

- Who in your life has supported you in your grief? How might you sincerely thank them or invite them into your healing process?
- Is there someone who didn't understand your loss? What would you want to say to them if you could speak freely and kindly?
- If you're in a family or partnership, how have you each experienced grief differently? What space can you make for each other's style?
- Could you invite others to remember your pet with you—through stories, shared photos, or even a quiet walk in their memory?

PART IV
LIVING WITH THE LOVE

CHAPTER 11
LIFE AFTER LOSS

You made it through the first half of the night. As for the first week, then. The month comes next. The house is quieter, but something is still missing; yet the stillness is not as pronounced as before. It has a warm and comforting quality. Even if the recollections continue to evoke strong feelings, they are occasionally accompanied by a grin rather than tears.

Life after the death of a pet does not mean that life will return to how it was before. It indicates that life starts to unfold around the place they had forgotten about. The ability to make dinner without stumbling over them at your feet is something you learn. As the night progresses, you find yourself sleeping without their warm body against yours. When you stop looking for their shadow in the hallway, you occasionally sense it even though you have stopped checking for it.

There is no end to grief. It progresses over time. As a result, it transforms from something overwhelming to something you bear. Unlike a wound, it is like a precious stone you carry in your pocket. It is always present. It can be pretty weighty. Grounding can occur at times. Reminding us of love at all times.

THERE IS NO "BACK TO NORMAL"

People frequently assume that there is a definitive period at which grieving ends and "normal" life begins when they discuss moving on. But if you have ever deeply loved a pet, you know there is no turning back. Your life was molded by the experiences you had with them. Your routines, your feelings, and even your identity were all altered as a result. Their absence leaves a mark behind. Further, what is to come is not a return to the previous state of affairs. It marks the beginning of a different experience.

You may still forget that they are no longer with you. You may grab the leash or the corner of the left-open bed. This does not mean that you are "stuck" in your habits. According to them, your love had a rhythm. It takes some time for rhythms to become free.

On the contrary, you start to construct something new rather than pursuing the usual. A regimen that does not include them but is influenced by their recollection. A life that still pays tribute to what they have bestowed upon you, even as you move forward into what is ahead.

THE BITTERSWEET RETURN OF JOY

When you laugh once again, you may find that you are experiencing a peculiar and unspoken sense of shame when you are having a day that is just wonderful. For example, when you find yourself laughing or dancing in the kitchen without thinking about it, you realize they are not present.

The instant you reach that point, grief will attempt to fool you. The voice asks, "How can you possibly be okay?" Have you failed to remember them? Laughter, however, is not the same thing as forgetting. It is therapeutic. It is your body's reminder that happiness is still attainable, even thereafter.

It is not true that joy absolves one of pain. That it has become more pliable. It indicates that your heart has widened to the point where it can accommodate both joy and grief. When you are joyful, you are not betraying your pet in any way. When all is said and done, they would want nothing more than for you to be happy. Your pain was never anything they asked for. It was as simple as showing love to one another repeatedly, and they would want you to do the same with yourself.

Letting Their Presence Live On

Even as their body is gone, your pet's presence can linger in the most unexpected places. It's a favorite song. A sunrise walk. The feel of fur on an old blanket. A memory triggered by the rustling of a treat bag. These small moments are invitations—not to ache, but to connect.

You may talk to them still. Whisper goodnight. Keep their photo nearby. These aren't signs that you're stuck in grief. These are signs that your love continues in the only way it now can: spiritually, emotionally, through memory, and through ritual.

You might even find comfort in creating a new bond—lighting a candle each night, journaling letters to them, or walking the route you once shared. These acts don't tether you to the past. They create a bridge between what was and what still is.

Rebuilding Routine and Purpose

After a pet dies, your daily routine often collapses. The feeding, walking, playing, cleaning—all of it vanishes in a day, leaving you unsure what to do with the time. The gaps in the day feel enormous. The structure of your world, once centered around caring for them, now needs to be rebuilt.

This transition can feel disorienting. But it can also be a gentle, slow opportunity to create new routines that nourish you. Not to replace them but to support the version of you that's emerging.

You might:

- Take a walk in their memory each morning or evening
- Start a gratitude journal, noting what brings peace each day
- Volunteer or support causes that mattered to you both
- Tend to a memorial space—lighting a candle, watering a plant
- Build in small joys—tea by the window, a daily poem, music

The routine doesn't erase grief. But it helps your nervous system regulate again. It brings moments of comfort, predictability, and even calm. In time, these new habits become threads in the new tapestry of your life.

RECONNECTING WITH PEOPLE AND THE WORLD

Grief has a way of making the world feel distant. After a pet loss, even social interaction can feel strange. Friends may not understand. Invitations may feel overwhelming. Laughter may feel like too much, too soon.

But slowly, when you're ready, the connection returns.

You may start with a call to someone who gets it. A walk with a neighbor. A visit to the place your pet loved. A conversation about them that brings more joy than tears.

Grief can deepen your empathy. You may find yourself more patient with others, more attuned to pain, and more drawn to authenticity. This sensitivity is a gift your pet helped shape. Let it guide you gently back into the world at your own pace.

WHEN SETBACKS HAPPEN

A wave can knock you off your feet when you think you're doing better. A scent, a sound, a season. Grief isn't linear, and setbacks are not failures. They're echoes.

It's okay to cry again. To miss them suddenly. To feel the pain come rushing back like it was yesterday. These waves don't mean you haven't healed. They tell you still love.

When a setback hits, breathe. Ground yourself. Speak to your pet. Write. Walk. Reach out. Do whatever you need to remind yourself: this wave will pass. You've survived before. You will again.

Becoming the Person They Saw in You

One of the most powerful ways to live after loss is to live as the person your pet believed you were. The one they looked at with adoration. The one who made them feel safe. The one who was enough—just as you are.

They saw your goodness. Your gentleness. Your strength. Your silliness. Your soul. Carry that forward.

Let their unconditional love become part of your inner voice. When you doubt yourself, hear their tail wag. When you feel lost, remember how they always found their way back to you. You are still that person. And now, you carry a piece of them wherever you go.

When You're Ready to Help Someone Else

Eventually, there may come a time when you feel the pull to support someone else. A friend is going through pet loss. A stranger in an online group. A child mourning a small animal for the first time.

You don't need expertise. You don't need to say the perfect words. Just your presence, empathy, and lived experience—that's enough.

Sitting beside someone in grief is one of the most powerful ways to honor your own. It transforms pain into purpose. It allows love to ripple outward again and again.

And If You're Not Ready Yet

That's okay. You don't need to rush. Life after loss isn't about proving resilience. It's about finding your way—at your own pace, in your way, with gentleness.

You are allowed to rest. You are allowed to remember. You can laugh and cry and feel empty and full on the same day.

There is no timeline for healing. There is only time—and love.

Reflections & Next Steps

- What part of your new routine brings you the most comfort, however small?
- What does joy look like now—and how can you invite more of it without guilt?
- If your pet could walk beside you today, what would they notice? How would they comfort you?
- Write a letter to yourself six months from now. What do you hope you've remembered, healed, or discovered?

CHAPTER 12
OPENING YOUR HEART AGAIN

Sometimes, it takes months, and sometimes, it takes years, but there comes a time when you hear a bark in the distance, see a pair of golden eyes at the shelter, or feel the brush of fur against your legs, and your heart begins to stir. Not in a state of agony but rather with a curious silence. Would it be possible for me to love once more?

The feeling of remorse then comes over you. The question is, "But what about them?" The voice asks, "Isn't this a little too soon?" And it leaves you unable to move forward or determine whether moving forward is a betrayal or a beginning. It leaves you paralyzed at the intersection of the past and the future.

After the passing of a cherished animal companion, one of the most profoundly personal choices you will ever have to make is whether or not to open your heart once again; a timetable is not available—no universal symbol. There is no easy answer. On the other hand, one thing consistent across all individuals is that your heart is still capable of love, not in place of the person you have lost, but because of them.

It is not the purpose of this chapter to instruct you on what to do. It is about assisting you in listening to your heart, understanding the feelings that come with making a choice once more, and ensuring you are reminded that expanding love does not entail abandoning someone.

The Myth of Replacement

One of individuals' most common concerns is that obtaining another pet will "replace" the one they have lost. That is a valid concern. The bond was one of a kind. Also, the sorrow is a holy thing.

Despite this, the truth is that love does not replace; instead, it increases.

Nobody can take the place of a soulmate. Be sure not to overlook your closest companion. You should make room for new companionship and do this when and if you are ready. This is not a copy. Not as a replacement for it. On the other hand, it is a fresh start, molded by the love you still hold within you.

Never two creatures are the same in any way. Their personalities, routines, peculiarities, and requirements will all be different. A portion of the beauty lies in that. We learn something fresh about love, patience, and ourselves from each pet.

The decision to open your heart again is not about trying to fill a hole in your life. Because you have experienced profound love in the past, it is essential to recognize and respect the ability of your heart to love again.

Guilt: The Guardian at the Door

People who are contemplating getting a new pet frequently experience feelings of guilt. The message reads, "How dare you move on so quickly?" It raises the question; would your pet be proud? When you can love again easily, it asks, "Do you even miss them?"

Conversely, guilt is not your guidance; rather, it is your sadness on display. Its goal is to shield you from experiencing any further discomfort. In its mind, loving again is synonymous with forgetting. To love again, however, is a necessary step toward healing.

Wouldn't you want your pet to be loved again if your positions were reversed and they had outlived you rather than vice versa? To enjoy delight, camaraderie, warm beds, and belly rubs? Your pet's love was never contingent on anything else. In addition to wagging their tails, purring, and chirping, they would express their approval by expressing a fundamental desire for you to be pleased.

You can say yes to love again, even though you will miss them forever. It is not disloyal to do so. This is a human thing.

QUESTIONS TO ASK BEFORE SAYING YES AGAIN

There's no "perfect" time to adopt or bring home a new animal. But there are questions worth sitting with, gently and honestly:

- Am I seeking a new pet to numb my pain—or to build something new?
- Do I have the emotional and physical energy to care for an animal right now?
- What type of personality, needs, or energy might best match my life now?
- How would I feel about their differences and similarities with my last pet?
- Have I created mental, physical, and emotional space for a new relationship to bloom?

These aren't tests you must pass. They're invitations to check in with yourself. You don't have to have it all figured out. You need to be willing to approach the process with love, honesty, and care.

GRIEVING AND BONDING AT THE SAME TIME

Some people expect that once they bring a new pet home, the grief will be "over." But what often happens is more complicated. You may love your new companion deeply—and still miss the one who came before. You may find yourself comparing them, resenting their differences, or aching for traits that aren't there.

This doesn't mean you made a mistake. It means you're human. You're building a new bond while still tending to the wounds of the last. That takes time, patience, and presence.

It's okay if it doesn't feel the same. It's OK if it takes time to connect. Let your new pet be themselves. Let your love unfold slowly. You're not building a replica—you're starting something entirely new.

When the Heart Says "Not Yet"

For some, the idea of bringing another pet home feels impossible. The grief is still fresh. The house still echoes with absence. The thought of going through loss again someday feels unbearable.

If that's where you are, that's okay. You are under no obligation to open your heart again. You don't need to "get back on the horse" or "start over." You don't need to adopt to prove anything—not even your love.

Sometimes, the greatest act of respect is letting the silence be sacred. Sometimes, healing looks like waiting, like grieving fully before welcoming something new. Listen to your timing. Trust it.

And know this: even if you never have another pet, your heart is still whole. It is still enough. It has already been loved deeply—and that, in itself, is legacy.

Other Ways to Reconnect Without Adopting

Opening your heart again doesn't always have to mean bringing a new pet home. Sometimes, it starts with softer steps—ways of reengaging with animals without fully committing to adoption.

Consider:

- Volunteering at a local shelter or rescue
- Fostering short-term for animals in transition

- Visiting therapy animals at hospitals, nursing homes, or schools
- Donating supplies or sponsoring an animal in your pet's name
- Pet-sitting for friends or family members
- Spending time in nature, watching birds, squirrels, or neighborhood dogs pass by

These small acts can help rebuild your connection to the animal world gently and on your terms. They keep your love alive without overwhelming your heart.

HONORING THE PAST WHILE WELCOMING THE FUTURE

If and when you welcome a new animal, create space for your grief and joy.

- Display a photo of your late pet in the home you share with the new one.
- Speak their name aloud when you remember them.
- Tell your new companion about the one who came before—how they paved the way for this love.
- Include small rituals: lighting a candle on the anniversary of your loss, sharing their story with others, and continuing traditions.

Let the past be part of the present. Let your new pet know they're not replacing anyone—they're being welcomed into a legacy of love.

LOVE DOESN'T END—IT EXPANDS

The heart is not a house with only one room. It's a cathedral. A garden. A sky. There is space for more than one love story.

Your pet didn't make love with them when they left. They left it with you. And what you do with that love now—that's up to you.

Your grief and love remain valid whether you open your door again, keep it gently closed, bring home a new friend, or smile at the neighbor's cat. There is no right way to move forward. There is only your way.

Trust your heart. It knows what it's doing.

Reflections & Next Steps

- What thoughts or emotions come up when you imagine loving a new pet? Do any surprise you?
- What would it say if your late pet could write you a note about loving again?
- What small steps—volunteering, visiting a shelter, even just walking past the dog park—feel manageable right now?
- If you welcome a new pet someday, what rituals might you create to honor the one who came before?

CHAPTER 13
KEEPING THE BOND ALIVE

D espite the passage of time, there is a part of you that remains in the same place—in the final moment, in the final farewell, in the way that they used to look at you as if you were their entire universe. You now carry them with you everywhere you go. It is not in your arms or on a leash but in your memory, your routine, and the unseen strands that continue to bind you together.

The fact that they are no longer physically present does not necessarily mean they have vanished. On the contrary, many bereaved pet owners discover that the link does not break after their companion's loss; instead, it transforms. It gets softer. It becomes more profound. It requests to be carried differently, but it prevails.

The act of clinging to the past or refusing to move forward is not what maintaining the connection means. At this point, it is essential to recognize that the relationship is still present but in a different form. The purpose of this chapter is to honor that fact and to create tiny, sacred ways to feel near to one another, even as life on earth continues.

LOVE DOESN'T DIE—IT EVOLVES

We continue to feel a connection to the person we love even after they have passed away. It goes from being something we can grab hold of to feeling intangible. This change might be challenging to manage when dealing with pets. Their affection was physical, akin to being crushed against our chests, curled up at our feet, and following us from one room to the next.

We long for their presence as soon as they are no longer here. However, what generally takes people by surprise is the amount that is still left. In your dreams, you might be able to hear them. During times of silence, you should feel them by your side. Feel them in the places that they cherished. You may reach for them without thinking, and even though your hand will touch the air, your heart will know that something is still there.

You are not engaging in wishful thinking. It is the process of mourning making its way to the memory. It is love adjusting to the experience of loss.

WRITING LETTERS TO YOUR PET

One of the most powerful ways to maintain your bond is to keep speaking to your pet. Writing letters allows your emotions—grief, gratitude, anger, joy, or longing—to flow. It turns pain into expression and memory into presence.

You might write:

- A thank-you note for the years you shared
- A reflection on what the day would've looked like if they were still here
- An update about your life, your healing, or your new routine
- An apology if something still weighs on you
- A note from them to you—what you imagine they'd say in return

These letters don't need to be shared or saved. They're for you and the love that endures. Some people write regularly—on anniversaries, birthdays, or when the ache resurfaces. Others keep a special journal just for these entries. However, you do it, writing can offer profound connection and peace.

CREATING RITUALS THAT KEEP THEM NEAR

Ritual gives grief a container. It offers your love a place to land. These small acts—repeated intentionally—can become part of carrying the bond forward.

Some healing rituals include:

- Lighting a candle each evening or on special dates
- Setting out a photo or collar in a dedicated space
- Wearing a piece of jewelry with their name, paw print, or birthstone
- Take a walk along your old route and say their name as you go
- Preparing their favorite treat or meal on a remembrance day and sharing it with another pet or friend
- Saying good morning or good night to them, aloud or silently

The rituals don't have to be big. They have to be honest. Let them evolve. Let them comfort. Let them remind you that the bond is still alive—even if your pet is not.

DREAM VISITATIONS AND SPIRITUAL PRESENCE

Many grieving pet parents report vivid dreams where their pet appears—healthy, joyful, peaceful. These dreams often have a sense of comfort, reunion, and even communication. Whether you believe these are visitations or creations of the subconscious, the effect is the same: you wake up feeling reconnected.

If you've had these dreams, write them down. Reflect on how they made you feel. What message did you take from them?

For some, these dreams come early in grief. For others, they arrive much later—when the heart is ready. And for some, they never come at all, and that's okay, too. You don't need a dream to know they love you. You are already living proof of that love.

Beyond dreams, some people describe feeling their pet's presence in daily life. A flash of movement, a shift in light, a warm feeling during a hard moment. These signs are not meant to be proven or explained. They're meant to be felt.

If you believe your pet is still nearby in spirit, trust that. Speak to them. Sit in silence and invite their memory forward. Let them be part of your spiritual landscape.

HONORING THEIR MEMORY THROUGH SHARED HABITS

Our pets shaped our daily lives. Their routines became ours. And when they're gone, those routines often unravel. But keeping one or two of those habits alive—adjusted for this new chapter—can be profoundly healing.

You might:

- Continue your morning coffee on the porch where you used to sit together
- Walk your favorite shared route and greet the trees you once passed
- Watch their favorite movie or show (yes, some pets had preferences!)
- Leave a spot open on the bed or couch
- Keep their name alive in conversations

These habits don't mean you're stuck. They tell you your love has rhythm—and you're still dancing to it in a new way.

CONNECTING THROUGH MUSIC, SCENTS, AND SENSORY MEMORY

Grief isn't only emotional—it's sensory. The smell of your pet's shampoo, the jingle of tags, the soft texture of their fur. These sensory memories can be powerful tools for keeping the bond alive.

Consider creating a sensory memory box:

- A swatch of their favorite blanket
- Their collar or a tag
- A toy or brush
- A vial of their scent or a shampoo they loved

- A recorded video or sound file of them playing or purring

You might also create a music playlist—songs that remind you of them or that played during essential moments. Listening to that playlist when you miss them becomes a kind of communion, a moment of closeness.

VISITING SHARED SPACES

Physical places carry memory. The dog park. The sunny windowsill. The hiking trail. The car seat. Once filled with energy and connection, these places may feel sacred or painful.

Revisiting them can be a meaningful way to reconnect.

You don't have to go with anyone. You don't have to stay long. Even standing at the edge of the space and saying their name can be powerful.

Bring something with you—an old photo, a flower, a note. Sit. Listen. Let the memory live.

Over time, these places shift. The pain softens, and the memory becomes richer. You may find yourself smiling there again. Not because you've moved on but because you're still in a relationship with your pet—just in a new, quieter way.

SIGNS, SYMBOLS, AND THE LANGUAGE OF GRIEF

Many people describe receiving "signs" from their pets—unusual animal sightings, specific numbers, songs on the radio, dreams, or moments that feel too meaningful to be coincidence.

Some people believe these are true messages. Others see them as the heart's way of noticing patterns that soothe. Either way, they offer comfort. They create a sense of presence. They invite trust.

If you notice these signs, honor them. Speak aloud. Say, thank you. Write them down. Let them be what they are: another way your bond continues.

You can even choose your symbol, which reminds you of your pet's spirit. A butterfly, a cloud, a paw print in the sand. Let it represent the invisible thread between you, still unbroken.

Your Pet's Legacy in Who You Are

Even if you do none of these rituals—even if you never light a candle, write a letter, or revisit a trail—your pet lives on in you.

In how you love.

In how you care for others.

In how you pause for the little things.

In the patience you learned.

In the softness you offer.

In the ways, your heart stretched just by knowing them.

That's the most profound bond—the legacy written into your soul.

You don't need to prove that the love continues. You are the proof.

Reflections & Next Steps

- What small ritual could you start this week to bring their memory gently into your day?
- Have you ever had a dream, sensation, or "sign" that reminded you of them? How did it make you feel?
- Write your pet a letter today. Tell them what life has been like without them. Tell them what you still carry.
- Create a "memory playlist" of songs reminding you of your bond. Listen to it when you need to feel close.

PART V
GUIDED REFLECTIONS
AND HEALING ACTIVITIES

CHAPTER 14
JOURNALING THROUGH THE JOURNEY

Experiencing grief is not always a linear process. You may feel stable one day, and then you may feel completely unhinged the next. During a peaceful morning, you can find yourself overcome with memories while you are at the grocery store, or you might be surprised by tears. Layers of memory are stored in the heart. Those layers often require more than thoughts and emotions; they need words. As a result, keeping a journal can become an invaluable resource.

Even though writing in a journal does not eliminate suffering, it provides a safe space to express it. You can think of it as a gentle container for feelings that are too huge, confused, or knotted to hold all by yourself. In addition, you do not need to be powerful to access those private pages. You don't need to be understood. But you need to be truthful.

This chapter encourages you to investigate journaling as a therapeutic tool, regardless of whether you have been writing for years or have never picked up a journal in your whole life. For the sake of eloquence. Aside from the answers. It is merely for presence. To be made available. It is for your memory.

WHY WRITING HEALS

Putting one's thoughts down on paper is a profound experience. Writing gives motion to the feelings of grief rooted in the body, whether tight in the chest or heavy in the stomach. The feeling is moved from the inside out by this sensation.

Keeping a journal is effective not because it is magical but rather because it is personal. You will be able to speak things you cannot say out loud. It enables you to revisit memories from the past safely. This becomes a conversation between your present and your past, as well as between your love and grief.

The formlessness of sadness is given structure through the act of writing. This, in and of itself, is a healing moment.

You Don't Have to Be a Writer

There's no right way to journal. You don't need perfect grammar or poetic flair. Your handwriting can be messy. Your words can be fragmented. You're not writing for anyone else. You're writing for the part of you that needs to speak without interruption.

You can:

- Write in full sentences
- Use bullet points
- Make lists of memories
- Doodle, sketch, or write poetry
- Repeat the exact words over and over
- Write one word if that's all you have

What matters isn't the style—it's the honesty. The permission to feel, however, shows up.

A Place for the Feelings That Don't Fit Elsewhere

Pet grief often comes with complicated emotions. One moment, you're full of love; the next, you're overwhelmed by guilt. Sometimes, you feel angry. Sometimes relieved. Sometimes, I am utterly numb.

Journaling permits you to name those feelings without judgment. You can write:

- "I miss you, and I'm mad at the world."
- "I wish I'd noticed the signs sooner."
- "You were the best thing in my life."
- "I don't know what to do with this pain."
- "I still feel you near me."

The page doesn't flinch. It doesn't correct you. It simply holds space.

Journaling as a Ritual of Connection

Writing can become a ritual you return to repeatedly to process grief and maintain the connection. Some people write letters to their pets. Others journal once a week, always lighting a candle or sitting in a particular chair.

Making writing part of your rhythm brings a sense of steadiness. Even when nothing else feels right, you can say, "This I will do. This page is mine."

Some people keep their pet's collar or photo nearby while they write. Others use a special journal set aside only for this grief. However, you do it, let it be a sacred pause in your healing.

Prompts to Help You Begin

If you're not sure where to start, begin with a prompt. These are open-ended invitations, not assignments. Let your heart lead. Write what comes. There are no wrong answers.

Here are **20 journaling prompts** to explore at your own pace:

1. What do I miss most about them today?
2. A memory I keep coming back to is...
3. If I could talk to them now, I'd say...
4. The moment I knew they were gone was...
5. My favorite silly habit of theirs was...
6. What I learned from loving them is...
7. If they could talk to me right now, they'd probably say...
8. I still feel them near me when...
9. A place that reminds me of them is...
10. I wish I could go back and...
11. I feel guilty about...
12. I forgive myself for...
13. A dream I've had about them...
14. The hardest part of the day is...
15. The thing I wish others understood is...
16. A funny memory that makes me smile is...
17. I want to remember them by...
18. On their birthday or adoption day, I plan to...
19. I've changed since losing them in these ways...
20. My heart feels most full when I...

You can return to these again and again. Sometimes, what you write will surprise you. Sometimes it will stay the same. All of it is valid.

SECTIONS TO STRUCTURE YOUR GRIEF JOURNAL

If you want to create a dedicated grief journal, consider organizing it by theme. This isn't necessary—but it can help you track your healing and revisit parts of your love when you're ready.

Here are a few sections you might include:

- Gratitude: Things you're thankful for about their life and your bond
- Guilt & Forgiveness: Space to process choices, regrets, and grace
- Favorite Memories: Stories, quotes, or moments you never want to forget
- Letters to Them: Messages written directly to your pet
- Dreams & Signs: Notes about moments when you felt them near
- Legacy & Growth: Reflections on how your pet shaped you and how you're honoring their memory

Each section can grow over time. There's no need to fill it all at once. Let it unfold as grief does—in its rhythm.

WHEN WRITING IS TOO HARD

Some days, the page will feel too heavy. You may sit down and find the silence unbearable. That's okay. Journaling is an invitation, not a requirement. On hard days, try this instead:

- Write one word that describes how you feel
- Draw a heart and whisper their name
- Light a candle and let the blank page be enough
- Reread an old entry and hold your own words gently

There is healing even in the pause.

Other Creative Ways to Journal

Journaling doesn't have to be only words. You can explore creative approaches that reflect your unique way of processing:

- Collage: Use cut-out images, photos, or stickers
- Art journaling: Blend watercolor, sketching, and writing
- Voice journaling: Record your thoughts as voice notes
- Video journaling: Speak into a camera and save your reflections privately

- Memory scrapbooking: Create a visual timeline of your pet's life

Whatever helps your heart speak—do that. Writing is only one voice. Grief listens to many.

THE JOURNAL AS A WITNESS TO YOUR LOVE

Perhaps the greatest gift of journaling is that it becomes a record of your love. Long after the rawness fades, these pages will remain. A living memory. A tribute.

Reading back months or years later, you'll see the arc of your healing. You'll remember things you thought you'd forgotten. You'll hear your voice—tender, truthful, trying.

And you'll realize this grief, love, and story mattered.

Reflections & Next Steps

- What kind of journaling feels most natural to you—words, lists, art, letters? Try that first.
- Set aside ten minutes today. Choose one prompt. Light a candle. Begin.
- What have you been holding in that might soften if you wrote it down?
- If your pet could read your journal, what do you hope they would feel?

CHAPTER 15
CREATIVE HEALING PROJECTS

Grief can be a noisy emotion, filled with tears, tangled thoughts, and deeply hurt questions. However, it is also possible for it to be quiet. It makes its way into your hands, the long silences of the day, and the part of you that used to be busied with activities such as brushing fur or cooking various meals. You could ask yourself, "What will I do with all this love now that I cannot give it to them?"

One solution is to engage in creative approaches to healing. They offer a destination for your affection. They provide a means for keeping your hands and your emotions involved with the memory of your pet in a way that is meaningful to you. You need not be sentimental, artistic, or crafty to do this. It is sufficient for you to be willing to express your sadness in a manner that turns it from a painful experience into a place of presence.

In this chapter, you will find various crafts based on memories and involving touch. Each of these projects is intended to assist you in remembering, honoring, and maintaining the connection you have with your pet. The process matters the most, regardless of whether you are making something tiny and personal or participating in an activity the whole family does together. Creating something flawless is not the goal here. It is about bringing something into existence.

THE COMFORT OF TANGIBLE CREATION

After loss, we often feel untethered. Routines vanish. Objects feel empty. Our hands, once busy caring for our pet, become still. Creative healing projects allow those hands to move again—with intention, care, and memory as their guide.

There's something deeply grounding about making a physical object that honors a relationship. Whether it's a memory box, a painting, a planted flower, or jewelry, these objects become anchors. They remind you of the love you shared. They offer comfort on days when grief feels especially raw.

Creating something can't bring them back—but it can bring you back to them in a tactile, nourishing, and healing way.

Memory Boxes: A Container for Love

A memory box is one of the simplest and most cherished healing projects. It doesn't require special materials or skills—just a box, some time, and the willingness to gather.

Start with a container that feels right to you. It can be:

- A wooden keepsake box
- Decorated cardboard or shoebox
- A small suitcase or drawer
- A handcrafted fabric pouch

Then, gently choose items to place inside. You might include:

- Their collar and tags
- A favorite toy or blanket
- Printed photos or Polaroids
- A lock of fur or whisker
- Their adoption papers or vet records
- Notes you've written to them
- Their name tag or paw print

Some people also include a small journal or letter-writing notebook tucked inside so they can continue the conversation. The box becomes a safe place—not just for items, but for emotions.

You can open it whenever you need to feel close. You can keep it somewhere private or display it as a tribute. It's yours, and there's no wrong way to build it.

DIY Pawprint Clay Keepsakes

If you have access to a pawprint—either taken by a vet after passing or one you did while your pet was still alive—you can create a beautiful clay keepsake. This small gesture becomes a touchable reminder of their physical presence.

Here's how to create one:

Materials:

- Air-dry clay or oven-bake clay
- Rolling pin
- Cookie cutter or circular mold (optional)
- A pencil or pointed tool
- Ribbon or string (if making an ornament)
- Acrylic paint (optional)

Steps:

1. Roll out the clay to about half an inch thick.
2. Press the pawprint gently into the clay (or use a mold or impression if pre-made).
3. Use a cutter or freehand shape around the print.
4. Use the tool to inscribe their name and the date.
5. Make a hole at the top if you want to hang it.
6. Let it dry thoroughly (air-dry or bake according to instructions).
7. Optionally, paint or seal the keepsake.

This small project becomes a piece of your pet's story—a timeless imprint of the love that walked beside you.

Painting or Sketching in Tribute

You don't have to be an artist to create something expressive and meaningful. Painting or drawing your pet can be a powerful act of remembrance, especially when done from the heart.

You can create:

- A complete portrait based on a favorite photo
- An abstract painting using colors that remind you of them
- A scene of their favorite place (under a tree, by the window, on your lap)
- A symbol that represents their spirit—a feather, a moon, a specific flower

If you're not confident in your drawing skills, consider using mixed media—collage, stamps, tracing, or digital art tools.

Making something or putting your pet's energy onto paper or canvas is more important than the final result. Let it be imperfect. Let it be honest. Let it be yours.

Creating a Garden or Living Tribute

Nature has a way of absorbing grief and returning peace. Planting something in your pet's memory can be both a grounding act and a growing legacy. Each season brings change, beauty, and reminders of life continuing.

Ideas for garden memorials:

- Plant a tree or shrub in your yard
- Create a small flower bed or potted plant display
- Place a stone with their name etched on it

- Add wind chimes, solar lights, or a small bench nearby
- Decorate the space with painted rocks or ceramic figures
- Scatter their ashes around a tree if meaningful

Tending to this living tribute can become part of your healing. Watering the flowers. Sitting in the shade. Watching butterflies or birds land nearby. These moments, quiet and sacred, say: They're still here in the breeze, the blooms, the beauty.

PERSONALIZED JEWELRY AND WEARABLE KEEPSAKES

Wearing something that reminds you of your pet can bring comfort throughout the day. It's like carrying a whisper of their spirit with you.

There are many types of memorial jewelry available, including:

- Lockets with a photo or a tiny fur clipping
- Bracelets engraved with their name or pawprint
- Ash-infused pendants
- Necklaces with their birthstone or a meaningful symbol (a star, feather, moon)
- Leather or fabric wrap bracelets with their tags incorporated

You can also make a custom piece or create your own using kits from online stores. Choose something that feels wearable and warm—not just in style but emotion.

SHARING THEIR STORY THROUGH A BOOK OR SCRAPBOOK

Sometimes, remembering your pet's story in full helps you see their life as a beautiful, complete arc—full of love, adventure, growth, and presence. Creating a scrapbook or storybook is a fantastic way to reflect and remember.

Sections might include:

- Their arrival (adoption or birth story)
- Favorite games and quirks
- Friends they made—human or animal
- Significant milestones (first trip, health recoveries, holidays)
- Messages from family and friends
- Final days and your goodbye
- Letters, poems, or quotes

This can be a profoundly personal keepsake or something shared with others, especially children in the family who grieved alongside you.

Candles and Scent Memory Projects

Scent is deeply tied to memory. Some people find healing in creating a candle or scent blend that reminds them of their pet. You can customize candles with essential oils, colors, or herbs that connect to your pet's personality.

A candle ritual might involve:

- Lighting it during reflection time or journaling
- Saying their name or a memory aloud
- Pairing it with music or silence
- Using it on anniversaries or holidays

You can even decorate the candle holder with their name or place it beside a framed photo.

These scent-based tributes engage your senses and create a ritual that helps hold their memory in a sensory, comforting way.

Creating Something with Others

If you're part of a family-shared household or friends who know your pet, consider doing a creative project together. This helps children, partners, or other pets feel part of the healing process.

You could:

- Paint rocks together with messages or images
- Bake a treat they love and enjoy it in their favorite spot
- Build a shadow box display
- Host a "memory night" and share stories while crafting together
- Plant a communal tree or garden with everyone contributing

Grief, when held together, becomes lighter. Creative projects make space for shared sorrow—and shared joy.

REFLECTIONS & NEXT STEPS

- What object, image, or space brings comfort when considering your pet? Could that inspire a creative project?
- Which healing projects in this chapter feel accessible now—memory box, garden, journal, candle, artwork?
- Invite someone into your creativity—ask a child to help decorate a box or a friend to walk with you as you choose a planting spot.
- Set a day this week to begin. Not to finish—to start. One step. One stroke. One small act of remembrance.

APPENDIX A
RESOURCES FOR SUPPORT

Grieving the loss of a pet can feel isolating—especially when the world doesn't always understand the depth of your pain. But you are not alone. Whether you need someone to talk to, a community that understands, or simply a place to read and reflect, support is out there.

This appendix lists resources that provide comfort, connection, and practical help. From hotlines and online communities to local support groups and spiritual guidance, these services remind you that your grief matters, and that healing is possible.

You don't have to walk this road alone.

24/7 Grief Support Hotlines (U.S. Based)

These hotlines are staffed with compassionate professionals and volunteers trained to support individuals dealing with pet loss and grief.

Pet Compassion Careline by Michelson Found Animals

1-855-245-8214 (Free of charge)
Offers 24/7 emotional support for pet loss, including euthanasia decisions and anticipatory grief.
www.foundanimals.org

ASPCA Pet Loss Hotline (Operated by Cornell University Veterinary School)

607-218-7457

Voicemail is available; trained volunteers return calls during support hours.

www.vet.cornell.edu

Lap of Love Pet Loss Support Line

855-352-5683

Offers compassionate support and also connects you with in-home euthanasia services and grief resources.

www.lapoflove.com

Online Pet Grief Support Groups and Communities

These virtual spaces offer connection, empathy, and a safe environment to share memories and emotions.

Pet Loss Support Group on Facebook

A private, moderated group with thousands of members worldwide. You can share photos and memories and receive support at any hour.

Search: Pet Loss Support Group on Facebook

- **Rainbow Bridge Pet Loss Grief Center**

  Offers forums, chat rooms, and a virtual memorial wall.
  www.rainbowsbridge.com

- **Grief Healing Discussion Groups (Hosted by Marty Tousley, RN)**

  Moderated online forums for pet loss and general grief. Warm, wise, and welcoming.
  www.griefhealingdiscussiongroups.com

In-Person Support Groups (Check Locally)

Many communities offer in-person grief support groups through:

- Veterinary schools or animal hospitals
- Local animal shelters or humane societies

- Churches, synagogues, or spiritual centers
- Grief counseling centers (sometimes offer pet loss-specific sessions)

Ask your veterinarian, local ASPCA, or spiritual leader for recommendations near you.

Websites Offering Grief Tools, Articles, and Guidance

- **Association for Pet Loss and Bereavement (APLB)**

  Educational articles, online chat rooms, certified grief counselors, and virtual memorials.

  www.aplb.org

- **The Ralph Site (UK-based but global reach)**

  Gentle, informative articles and peer support forums written by grieving pet parents and veterinary professionals.

  www.theralphsite.com

- **Pet Loss Help**

  A central hub with resourcc lists, books, and coping tools.

  www.pet-loss.net

Faith-Based and Spiritual Resources

No matter your beliefs, you may find solace in practices that help you connect to something greater—God, nature, spirit, or the mystery of life and death.

- **Animal Chaplains and Interfaith Pet Blessings**

  Many churches and temples offer blessings for animals or pet memorials, especially around St. Francis Day (October 4). Reach out to a spiritual leader for guidance or comfort.

- **OneSpirit Interfaith Ministers Directory**

  Some ordained ministers specialize in animal chaplaincy and grief care.

- **Center for Spirituality and Healing – University of Minnesota**

  Provides guided meditations, healing rituals, and grief practices rooted in wellness and spiritual care.
  www.csh.umn.edu

WHEN PROFESSIONAL SUPPORT FEELS RIGHT

Sometimes, grief is layered, prolonged, or connected to other life challenges. If you're feeling stuck, overwhelmed, or isolated, speaking with a licensed mental health professional can help.

Search for:

- Therapists specializing in pet loss (PsychologyToday.com allows you to filter by specialty)
- Grief counselors with training in companion animal loss
- Teletherapy platforms offering grief support via phone or video

If you ever feel that your grief is leading to hopelessness or emotional despair, please seek professional help. Your pain is not a burden—it's a signal that your heart needs tending.

There is no single right way to grieve. There is only your way. And whatever path you're walking—whether it's with ritual, writing, silence, prayer, or creation—hands are willing to hold yours.

These resources exist to walk beside you. To remind you that love doesn't end here. To affirm that your pet's life matters, and so does your healing.

Let them be a bridge. Let them guide you back toward comfort, hope, and connection.

APPENDIX B
BOOKS AND TOOLS FOR KIDS

For many children, the death of a beloved pet is their first real encounter with loss. A friend who never judged them, greeted them after school, or listened without speaking is suddenly gone—and they may not yet have the language to describe what they're feeling.

But even without words, their hearts know something is missing.

Children grieve differently than adults. Their sadness may appear in brief bursts, sudden questions, unusual behavior, or quiet withdrawal. They may cry one moment and laugh the next. They may seem fine—until bedtime, or a holiday, or a memory stirs the ache again.

This appendix offers thoughtful tools and resources to help children feel seen, heard, and supported. It includes book recommendations, creative activities, and words that can make difficult conversations easier.

Whether you're a parent, grandparent, teacher, or family friend, your presence, honesty, and love will shape how the child learns to carry this grief—and how they continue to love with an open heart in the future.

BOOKS THAT HELP CHILDREN UNDERSTAND AND PROCESS PET LOSS

These titles offer age-appropriate stories and gentle explanations to help children explore grief, emotions, and the concept of saying goodbye.

The Rainbow Bridge: A Visit to Pet Paradise by Adrian Raeside

It is a tender, comforting picture book about what happens to pets after they die, with gentle humor and heartwarming illustrations.

The Tenth Good Thing About Barney by Judith Viorst

It is a classic story in which a young boy honors his cat by listing ten good things about him. Thoughtful and bittersweet, it is perfect for early elementary readers.

When a Pet Dies by Fred Rogers

From the beloved Mr. Rogers, this book explains death and the following feelings with simple language, photos, and warmth.

Saying Goodbye to Lulu by Corinne Demas

It is a story about a girl and her aging dog. Honest and beautifully written, it gently walks through illness, death, and remembrance.

Goodbye, Brecken by David Lupton

Illustrated with softness and care, this book helps children feel seen in their sadness and encourages open conversations about pet loss.

The Invisible Leash by Patrice Karst

The author of The Invisible String, this book comforts children by reinforcing the idea that the bond with a lost pet continues, even if they are no longer physically present.

I'll Always Love You by Hans Wilhelm

A sweet story about a boy who shares how much he loved his dog and how saying "I love you" every day helps him through the goodbye.

Coloring Books and Activity Journals

For children who process emotions better through play or art, these resources offer calming, creative ways to work through grief:

Healing Hearts: A Coloring Book for Grieving Children by Amy T. Wolpert

Simple, expressive images and gentle prompts help children understand and express their emotions.

My Pet Memory Book: For Children Grieving the Loss of a Pet by DeeDee Cummings

An interactive memory journal where children can draw, write, and talk about their pet, what they miss, and what they remember.

Remembering My Pet: A Kid's Own Spiritual Workbook for When a Pet Dies by Nechama Liss-Levinson

This Jewish faith-based workbook is adaptable for all spiritual backgrounds and includes rituals, reflections, and storytelling activities.

Memory Box Activities for Children

Creating a memory box is a simple yet powerful project that gives kids a hands-on way to honor their pets. Together, you can gather:

- Photos
- A drawing or handwritten note to their pet
- A collar or tag
- A lock of fur
- A small toy or treat they loved
- A rock or object from their favorite park or backyard
- A scent—like a sachet with lavender or their favorite shampoo

Let the child decorate the box. Use stickers, markers, paint—whatever helps them express themselves. This box can be kept on a shelf or opened on special days. It's a treasure chest of love.

Language That Helps: Words for Difficult Moments

Children often take emotional cues from the adults around them. You don't need all the answers; you must speak honestly, warmly, and simply.

Here are a few examples of language that may help:

- "It's okay to feel sad. I feel sad, too."
- "They died, which means their body stopped working. It doesn't hurt anymore, but we still miss them very much."
- "You can still talk to them if you want to. You can tell them you love them whenever you need to."
- "Do you want to draw something about them?"
- "We're going to feel lots of different things. That's normal. All feelings are okay."
- "Let's light a candle or make something special to remember them."

Avoid phrases like "went to sleep," which can confuse or scare children. If you have spiritual beliefs, you can share them with care, always making space for the child's questions and interpretations.

Support for Parents and Caregivers

If you're supporting a child through pet loss, remember to take care of yourself too. Grief is layered, and children often feel your emotions even when you don't speak them aloud.

It's okay for them to see you cry. It teaches them that sadness is safe, and love is real.

You might also consider:

- Reading a book together at bedtime that comforts both of you
- Scheduling quiet time each day to check in or talk about memories
- Talking to a counselor if grief brings up other emotional challenges

- Joining a pet loss group that welcomes children and families

Your love, consistency, and presence will stay with them forever—just like the pet they're learning to live without.

Grieving a pet teaches children something profound: that love is worth the sorrow. That goodbye doesn't mean the love is gone. And their memories, rituals, stories—they all matter.

Let them cry. Let them play. Let them draw and talk and run and pause.

Let them grieve like only children can—open-hearted and unfiltered.

And most of all, let them know they're not alone.

APPENDIX C
AFTERCARE
AND MEMORIAL SERVICES

S aying goodbye to a beloved pet doesn't end with their passing. For many, the question comes quietly and painfully in the following hours or days: What do I do now? Choosing aftercare options—burial, cremation, memorials—is never easy, especially when your heart is still in shock.

This chapter is here to walk beside you through that part of the journey. It gently lays out your options and offers suggestions for meaningful ways to honor your pet's life. Whether you want a private backyard ceremony, a custom urn, or a digital tribute that lives forever online, you'll find guidance here to help you decide what feels right—for your heart, pet, and memories.

There is no one "correct" way to say goodbye. What matters most is that your choices reflect your love and offer comfort in the coming days and years.

Burial Options

If you prefer to lay your pet to rest in a physical space, you have several options depending on where you live and what your local laws allow.

Home Burial

Some families choose to bury their pets at home—usually in a backyard or private property. Before doing this, check local regulations, as not all municipalities allow pet burial.

If permitted, choose a peaceful spot that is meaningful. You may:

- Wrap your pet in a favorite blanket or biodegradable shroud
- Bury keepsakes like a toy, letter, or photo
- Create a marker—a stone, plaque, or handmade sign
- Plant flowers, a bush, or a tree as a living memorial

This can be a profoundly healing ritual, especially for children, as it allows for ceremony and closure in a familiar setting.

Pet Cemeteries

Dedicated pet cemeteries offer burial plots, headstones, and ongoing care. Many also provide visitation areas and hold annual remembrance ceremonies.

Services often include:

- Transportation of your pet
- Preparation and casketing
- Headstone engraving
- Perpetual grounds maintenance

Ask your vet or about the local humane society, or search online to find one nearby.

CREMATION OPTIONS

Cremation is one of the most common and accessible forms of pet aftercare. It allows you to keep, scatter, or share your pet's remains meaningfully.

Individual or Private Cremation

Your pet is cremated alone, and you receive only their ashes. This option is ideal if you wish to keep or bury the remains in a personal urn.

Communal Cremation

Multiple pets are cremated together. No ashes are returned. This is typically a more affordable option, and some facilities offer scattering in a memorial garden.

Most veterinary offices work with trusted cremation services and can help coordinate your arrangements. Be sure to ask:

- How the cremation is performed
- Whether you'll receive your pet's ashes
- What type of urn or container will be provided
- What memorial options are available (paw prints, fur clippings, certificates)

URNS, MEMORIAL CONTAINERS, AND KEEPSAKES

If you choose cremation, you can store your pet's ashes in an urn or memorial item—these range from elegant and straightforward to personalized and unique.

Common urn styles include:

- Wooden boxes (with engravings or photo slots)
- Ceramic or metal urns with paw prints
- Biodegradable urns for burial or water scattering
- Small keepsake urns (to divide ashes among family members)

You can also find custom memorial items that incorporate ashes, such as:

- Glass-blown beads or orbs
- Jewelry (lockets, rings, bracelets)
- Resin art or framed shadowboxes

Choose what brings you comfort. If you're unsure, many families temporarily store ashes in a simple container until they're ready to decide.

Scattering Ashes and Natural Memorials

Some people choose to scatter their pet's ashes in meaningful places:

Popular locations include:

- A backyard or garden
- A favorite walking trail or park
- Along a beach or shoreline
- Near a tree, flowerbed, or memorial bench

If scattering in public, be respectful and check any local rules or environmental guidelines. Choose a calm day and consider saying a few words or reading a poem as part of the moment.

You can also scatter some ashes and keep the rest in a keepsake urn or vial.

Digital and Printed Pet Obituaries

Your pet's story is worth sharing. Writing an obituary or tribute can help you process your grief, celebrate your life, and preserve memories for years.

A pet obituary might include:

- Their full name or nickname(s)
- Adoption or birthdate
- Personality traits (quirks, favorite toys, funniest moments)
- Their favorite activities and places
- The impact they had on your life
- A message from you or your family
- Details of a memorial service (if any)

You can post this:

- On social media or pet grief forums
- As part of a printed photo book or scrapbook

- On a memorial site like Rainbow Bridge or Pet Heaven
- In a keepsake journal or letter collection

These stories become part of your healing. They allow you to remember how your pet passed and how they lived.

CREATING ONGOING TRADITIONS

Memorializing your pet isn't a one-time event. It's something you may return to again and again in small, loving ways.

You might:

- Please light a candle on the anniversary of their passing
- Donate to a shelter in their name
- Create a photo book or slideshow
- Hold a remembrance walk or picnic
- Display their collar or photo in a special place

These rituals keep their memory woven into your life. They bring warmth on hard days and invite connection when you miss them most.

Aftercare is not just about logistics. It's about love. It's about how you choose to say goodbye—and how you begin to carry that goodbye forward.

Whether you keep their ashes on a shelf or plant a tree in their honor, hold a quiet ceremony, or tell their story to friends, meaning matters most. Not perfection. Not rules, which means.

You've already given them a life filled with love. Now, you get to honor that love in whatever way brings you peace.

CLOSING REFLECTION
WHERE LOVE GOES NOW

Every once in a while, in an unassuming and quiet way, the most challenging aspect of grieving begins to lessen. Perhaps at first, you won't even notice it. You might still shed tears whenever their name is mentioned or hesitate when you walk by where their bed used to be. The situation, however, has changed. Your agony, which was once severe and unrefined, is no longer the only thing you are experiencing.

Gratitude begins to permeate your entire being. You now feel a gentle warmth in the place where there was once only pain. It's no longer just the loss you remember but the life that came before it. Not just the farewell but the countless moments that led up to it.

The purpose of this book was never to alleviate your sorrow. The purpose of this was never to rush you or tell you what the healing process "should" look like. It was here to walk alongside you, one page at a time, one breath at a time, until your love became more potent than your sadness.

You have come a very long way.

You have sat with tears and memories in your eyes. Your pet has been honored through rituals, reflections, creative expression, and care. You have been through the starting days, the ones that were the most difficult and those that didn't make any sense. You've carried a connection that is so profound and so genuine that it could not be severed by death.

Even now, that connection is still with you.

THEY CHANGED YOU—AND THAT'S FOREVER

Our pets come into our lives without conditions. They don't ask for explanations or credentials. They don't need us to be perfect. They only need our presence. And in return, they offer something pure: a love so consistent, so unfiltered, that it quietly rewires who we are.

Maybe you became more patient. Perhaps you laughed more. Maybe you learned to slow down. Maybe you found strength you didn't know you had when you cared for them during illness. Perhaps you discovered a new kind of vulnerability when you completely let them into your heart.

These are not small things.

These are legacies.

You are what remains long after the leash has been put away, after the food bowl has been stored, and after the sympathy cards have stopped arriving. You, carrying the lessons they taught, the love they gave, and the joy they sparked. You walked forward in a world with beauty, meaning, and room for laughter, even in loss.

THE WORLD MAY NOT ALWAYS UNDERSTAND—BUT YOU KNOW

Pet grief is often misunderstood. The world may not always offer the same compassion it gives to other kinds of loss. You may have encountered that—well-meaning comments, uncomfortable silences, or outright dismissal of your pain.

But you know the truth. You know what they meant to you. You know how real the bond was. You see the shape of the silence they left behind.

Let that be enough.

You don't need the world's validation to grieve deeply. You already have the evidence of love in every memory, every photo, every whisper of their name.

You know.

YOU STILL GET TO TALK ABOUT THEM

Your pet's story didn't end with their death. It continues through you.

You can speak their name. Tell their stories. Show their photos. Laugh at their quirks. Describe their habits to someone new. You can let their memory breathe.

There is no expiration date on remembrance.

You may meet someone years from now who never knew them. And when you talk about your pet, they'll see your eyes light up and learn this was someone who mattered.

So, speak of them often. Let their love live through your words.

WHERE LOVE GOES NOW

You may still be figuring out how to live without their physical presence. That's okay. Some answers come slowly. Some never come at all. But love doesn't end—it shifts. It settles into the space between the breaths. It finds new expressions. It walks beside you like a shadow on a warm day—soft, subtle, constant.

Love goes into the way you care for others. Into the way, you pause and listen. Into the walks you take, the animals you support, the quiet moments when you sit by the window and feel something familiar in the light.

Love goes into healing. Into honoring. Into remembering.

And eventually, into loving again—not to replace what was lost, but to allow your heart to expand once more.

You Are Not Alone

As you close this book, know you're part of something bigger. Others have walked this path. Others have cried in the middle of the night, saved a favorite toy, written letters, planted trees, and lit candles.

You are one of us now.

A keeper of stories.

A witness to unconditional love.

A soul brave enough to grieve deeply because you dared to love fully.

That is no small thing. That is everything.

Your Story Continues

You will never forget them. And you shouldn't have to.

The chapters ahead will look different. Some will still carry sorrow. Others will have joy. Many will take both. But woven through them all is the thread of a love that shaped you—and still shapes you.

So let this be your quiet permission:

To laugh again.

To cry again.

To love again.

To live in a way that honors what you shared—and to keep that bond alive for as long as you need.

Because goodbye isn't the end of the story.

It's simply the beginning of loving them in a new way.

Always.